Hello and welcome!

AF238538

Nachdem du neue Wörter in der Schule besprochen hast, kannst du die **New words** in diesem Buch als Vokabelheft benutzen.

Hello and welcome!
Ich bin der Wordmaster und helfe dir beim Wörterlernen.

Die **fett gedruckten** deutschen Wörter sind Lernwörter. Sie fehlen im englischen Satz, damit du sie eintragen kannst.

ction **1**

Meine Tipps

1 Die Reihenfolge der **New words** entspricht der Reihenfolge der neuen Wörter im Vocabulary deines Schülerbuches. Dort kannst du deine Lösungen überprüfen.

2 Wenn du mal nicht weiter weißt, kannst du auch im Vocabulary nachschauen.

3 Lern neue Wörter in einem Satz. So kann man sie sich besser merken.

4 Üb den neuen Wortschatz. Deck zum Beispiel mit einem Blatt Papier die englischen Sätze ab und versuch, die deutschen Sätze ins Englische zu übersetzen. Oder umgekehrt.

New words ▸ p. 1

Mein **Name** ist …	My <u>name</u> is …
Ich komme aus Deutschland.	<u>I'm from</u> Germany.
Ich gehe zur **Schule**.	I go to <u>school</u> .
Ich **lerne** Englisch.	I _____ English.
Unser **Lehrer** ist nett.	Our _____ is nice.

… das große R bedeutet Revision: Auf Deutsch Wiederholung. Hier übst du Vokabeln, die du bereits früher gelernt hast.

Hi! Ich bin Ken und gebe dir Tipps. Zum Beispiel …

Überhaupt: Es gibt neben **New words** viele lustige Übungen. Die Lösungen findest du im beigelegten Heftchen.

Introduction

New words ▶ *pp. 6 – 7*

Wir haben viel Spaß in unserer **Jugend**gruppe.	We have lots of fun in our _____ group.
Welche Bands spielen auf dem **Fest**?	Which bands are playing at the _____ ?
Ist Wales ein Teil des **Vereinten Königreiches**?	Is Wales part of the _____ ?
Wir trafen Menschen **aus der ganzen Welt**.	We met people _____ .
Magst du diese **Art von** Musik?	Do you like this _____ music ?
Dieser Fußballstar ist ein **National**held.	This football star is a _____ hero.
Magst du wirklich **klassische** Musik?	Do you really like _____ music?
Ja, und ich gehe oft zu **Konzerten**.	Yes, and I often go to _____ .
Legt Rob jedes Wochenende **Platten auf**?	Does Rob _____ every weekend?
Aus welchem Land kommt das **Steeldrum**?	What country is the _____ from?
Man braucht **Stahl** um Brücken zu bauen.	You need _____ to build bridges.
Ich kann **Schlagzeug** und **Fiedel** spielen.	I can play the _____ and the _____ .
Übrigens habe ich mir eine Gitarre gekauft.	_____ , I've bought a guitar.
Im **Norden** ist es meistens kälter.	It's usually colder in the _____ .

1 Crossword

Across

2 Sue loves singing. She'd like to be a ★ in a band. (6)
4 great, super, very good (9)
6 I like this band best. It's my ★ band.(9)
8 –What can I do at the festival today?
– Look at the ★. It has all the information. (9)
10 What instrument do you ★ (4)
11 Linda is the star of our ★. (4)
12 You need one to get into the theatre or cinema. (6)

Down

1 You sing it. (4)
2 a famous singer, actor. etc. (4)
3 TAURIG: You can find an instrument in these letters. (6)
4 Maybe one day I'll be rich and ★. (6)
5 practise for a show, concert, etc. (8)
7 You often hear this instrument in churches. (5)
8 This instrument has a black and white keyboard. (5)
9 Nice to listen to: people sing it or play it on instruments. (5)

New words ▸ *pp. 8 – 9*

Wir verbrachten die Woche in einer **Herberge**.	We spent the week at a _____ .
Frag mich nicht. Ich bin nicht der **Chef**.	Don't ask me. I'm not the _____ .
Unsere Band **hat** jeden Monat **einen Auftritt**.	Our band _____ every month.
eine **Mischung** aus Jazz und klassischer Musik	a _____ of jazz and classical music
Wir spielen nicht nur **westliche** Musik.	We don't just play _____ music.

2 Verb forms

Ergänze die Tabelle der unregelmäßigen Verben.

1	*keep*	*kept*	kept
2		showed	
3	spend		
4	hide		
5		did	
6			taken

7	fly		
8		read	
9			thrown
10			spoken
11		wrote	
12	ride		

3 Lost words

Ergänze die Sätze mit den Wörtern im Feuerwerk.

1 _____ his youth grandpa was a very good swimmer.

2 What kind _____ music do your parents like?

3 People _____ all over Germany came to the concert.

4 What's the shortest way _____ the hostel?

5 There were three different bands _____ the gig.

6 _____ the way, where did you buy the steel drum?

7 B comes _____ C in the alphabet.

8 And D comes _____ C and E.

9 Why don't we meet _____ Wednesday?

10 London is famous _____ its pop concerts.

11 My father is _____ two metres tall.

(Feuerwerk: from, in, by, between, of, before, to, on, for, over, at)

New words   ▶ pp. 10 – 11

Warst du jemals in den **Vereinigten Staaten**?   Have you been to the _____ ?

Ich habe Hunger. – **Wie wär's mit** einer Pizza?   I'm hungry. – _____ a pizza?

Hast du im **Workshop** viel gelernt?   Did you learn much at the _____ ?

Nett, dich kennenzulernen.   _____ .

Eine halbe Stunde später kam er.   He came _____ later.

Er gab mir die **Hälfte** seiner Brote.   He gave me _____ of his sandwiches.

Lass uns **in Verbindung bleiben**.   Let's _____ .

Wird Tim auf der Party sein?– **Wart's ab!**   Will Tim be at the party? – _____

eine neue **Aufnahme** eines alten Lieds   a new _____ of an old song

Welches Bild **passt zu** welchem Wort?   Which picture _____ which word?

Kannst du **elektrische** Gitarre spielen?   Can you play the _____ guitar?

Spielst du **Querflöte** oder **Blockflöte**?   Do you play the _____ or the _____ ?

Wann hat er angefangen **Saxophon** zu spielen?   When did he start to play the _____ ?

Ist dies eine **Trompete** oder eine **Posaune**?   Is this a _____ or a _____ ?

Auf diese Weise ist es einfacher.   It's easier _____ .

die beste **Art und Weise**, eine Sprache zu lernen   the best _____ to learn a language

4   Last letter – first letter

Der letzte Buchstabe von jedem Wort ist gleichzeitig der erste des nächsten Wortes.

1   Trommel
2   Mischung
3   elektrisch
4   Konzert
5   Trompete
6   Posaune
7   genug
8   Hälfte
9   Fiedel
10   Aufzug (AE)
11   Blockflöte

5 Word search

Finde und markiere die 10 Musikinstrumente im Gitter. Gib dann ihre deutschen Übersetzungen an. (↓ →)

W	Y	H	D	T	K	X	Z	L	N
M	Y	Q	R	T	K	K	W	M	R
J	O	O	U	F	I	D	D	L	E
T	R	O	M	B	O	N	E	F	C
P	T	R	U	M	P	E	T	L	O
I	C	G	N	H	F	B	D	U	R
A	Z	A	P	U	R	T	M	T	D
N	V	N	U	U	H	P	Z	E	E
O	G	U	I	T	A	R	B	K	R
S	A	X	O	P	H	O	N	E	Y

drum – Trommel

_____   _____

_____   _____

_____   _____

_____

6 Word groups

*Trage die Wörter von der Wiese
in die richtigen Kletterseile ein.*

clothes

jobs

places in town

animals

engineer   dress   deer   department store   fireman   frog   hedgehog   hospital   hostel
jacket   leisure centre   mole   paramedic   photographer   police station   policewoman
pyjamas   restaurant   sandals   skirt   squirrel   trousers   waiter   woodpecker

Unit 1

New words ▸ p. 12

London ist die **Hauptstadt** von Großbritannien.   London is the _____ of Great Britain.

Die Aussicht vom **Riesenrad** ist toll.   The view from the _____ is fantastic.

Schau, dieses Auto hat nur drei **Räder**.   Look. This car has only got three _____ .

Hohe Gebäude haben meistens einen Fahrstuhl.   _____ buildings usually have a lift.

Touristen lieben die **Sehenswürdigkeiten**.   Tourists love the _____ .

Wie heißt das deutsche **Parlament**?   What's the name of the German _____ .

eine **Tondatei** kopieren   copy a _____

Obwohl wir gut spielten, verloren wir.   _____ we played well, we lost.

Lebt die **königliche** Familie in diesem Schloss?   Does the _____ family live in this castle?

Manchmal kann man die **Königin** sehen.   Sometimes you can see the _____ .

Im Sommer gibt es Konzerte **im Freien**.   In summer there are _____ concerts.

Sie warf den Ball hoch in die **Luft**.   She threw the ball high in the _____ .

Hast du letzte Nacht von mir **geträumt**?   Did you _____ about me last night?

1 Definitions

Vervollständige die Definitionen mit Wörtern aus den Mauersteinen. Trage die richtigen Wörter aus Kens Zeitung in die rechte Spalte ein.

wheels
capital
sights

queen
hostel
concert

| important | hotel | country | four | photos | | |
| spend | stage | king | move | places | live | woman |

1 A car needs them to _mOve_ and usually has _____ of them.   *wheels*

2 the most _____ city in a _____   _____

3 interesting _____ in a city: tourists often take _____ of them   _____

4 an important _____ , often the wife of a _____   _____

5 a place to _____ the night, usually cheaper than a _____   _____

6 _____ music, usually on a _____ , for people to enjoy   _____

New words   ▸ *p. 13*

Im **Naturkunde**museum können wir   At the _____ museum we can

... etwas über **Dinosaurier** lernen.   ... learn something about _____ .

Beim **Erdbeben** starben viele Menschen.   Many people died in the _____ .

die Geschichte des Lebens auf der **Erde**   the history of life on _____

einen **schicken** Rock kaufen   buy a _____ skirt

Kleider **aus zweiter Hand** sind oft billig.   _____ clothes are often cheap.

Isst du oft indische **Gerichte**?   Do you often eat Indian _____ ?

Lamm finde ich lecker.   I think _____ is delicious.

gute **Tipps**, wie man Geld sparen kann   good _____ about how you can save money

2   Crossword: places in a city

Die Buchstabenrätsel helfen dir, die Lösungen zu finden. (↓ →)

Across

1 ISOPHTAL: You can get help here if you're ill. (8)
4 EUUMMS: Go to this place to see old and interesting things. (6)
5 KCLO: a kind of lift for boats (4)
7 CAPELA: Kings and queens live here. (6)
9 DALERCATH: a very important church (9)
11 MOLCUN There's a statue of Nelson on top of one. (6)

Down

2 KRAP: Go here to walk, relax or play. (4)
3 SERQUA: a place with buildings on four sides (6)
5 RIBALRY: You can find lots of books here. (7)
6 RUCHCH: a building, often with a tower – some people go there on Sundays (6)
8 SICCUR: a round place with buildings around it (6)
10 NALE: a kind of road (4)

3   One or two letters?

Trage die fehlenden Buchstaben ein:
d *oder* **dd**, **f** *oder* **ff**, **n** *oder* **nn**.

d   dd   fi____le, mi____le , stu____ent, hi____en, rea____y, mo____el

f   ff   a____raid, gira____e, tra____ic, o____ten, di____icult, le____t

n   nn   a____orak, begi____ing, di____er, tu____el, e____emy, pe____cil

New words ▸ pp. 14–15

Drei **einfache Fahrkarten** kosten mehr

Three _____ cost more

... als eine **Tagesfahrkarte**.

... than a _____ .

öffentliche Verkehrsmittel benutzen

use _____

Es gibt viel Verkehr in der **Hauptverkehrszeit**.

There's lots of traffic in the _____ .

Wir brauchen eine Fahrkarte für zwei **Zonen**.

We need a ticket for two _____ .

In London fahre ich immer mit der **U-Bahn**.

In London I always travel by _____ .

Fahren alle **Linien** in die Stadtmitte?

Do all _____ go to the city centre?

Nimm die Victoria Line **in Richtung Norden**.

Take the Victoria Line _____ .

Ihr müsst am Piccadilly Circus **umsteigen**.

You have to _____ at Piccadilly Circus.

Unser Zug fährt vom **Bahnsteig** 2.

Our train goes from _____ 2.

die Hauptstädte von **Mittel**europa besuchen

visit the capitals of _____ Europe

Ich **horchte auf**s Telefon, aber es klingelte nicht.

I _____ the phone, but it didn't ring.

Ich kann mir nicht so viele **Einzelheiten** merken.

I can't remember so many _____ .

Früher einmal war hier eine Brücke.

_____ there was a bridge here.

Wo kann man heute **über** den Fluss gehen?

Where can you go _____ the river today?

4 Word ladder

Gehe von unten nach oben, indem du bei jeder Sprosse einen Buchstaben veränderst.

milk · · · · · · · · · · have

Do you take ★ in your tea?

1.6 km = 1 ★.

This pen isn't ★? Is it yours?

good, OK

Which underground ★ can I take to the cathedral?

We live in the little house at the end of this ★.

the opposite of 'early'

The flight leaves from ★ 14.

the opposite of 'love'

I'm staying in bed today because I ★ a cold.

5 More about ... London Underground

Vervollständige den Text mit den Wörtern aus der Box.

also although and
because before but
more only too when

London Underground is the oldest underground railway in the world. People _also_ (1) call it the 'Tube'

_____ (2) the tunnels look like *tubes. The first line opened in 1863. It was _____ (3) six

kilometres long. The first electric trains came in 1890; _____ (4) that, there were *steam trains.

Today there are 12 lines _____ (5) 275 stations. Together all the lines are 408 kilometres long,

_____ (6) only 185 kilometres are actually under the ground. Outside the city centre, the lines run

over ground _____ (7). In 1863, _____ (8) the Underground opened, 41,000 people travelled

on the first day. Today _____ (9) than 3 million people use the Tube every day. _____ (10) it's

more expensive than the bus and you don't see as much of London, it's the fastest way to travel around

the city.

tube = Röhre; steam train= Dampfzug

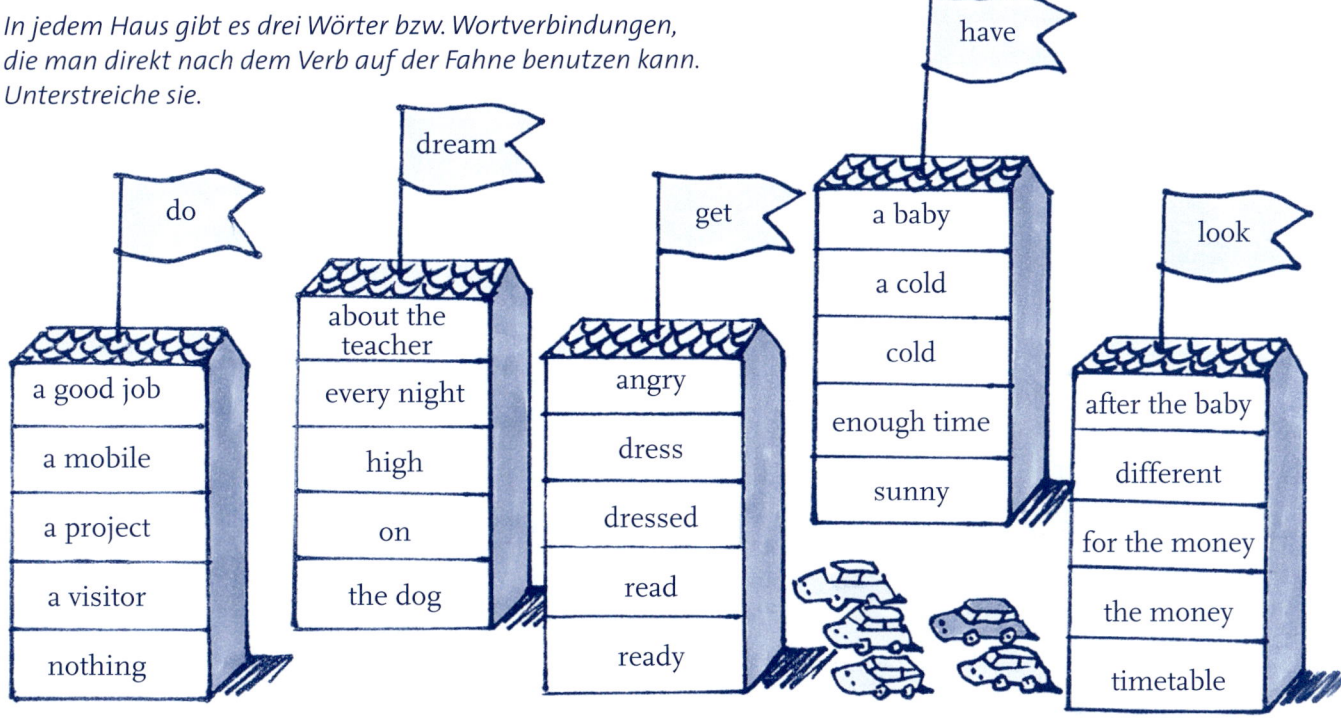

6 Word friends

*In jedem Haus gibt es drei Wörter bzw. Wortverbindungen,
die man direkt nach dem Verb auf der Fahne benutzen kann.
Unterstreiche sie.*

do
a good job
a mobile
a project
a visitor
nothing

dream
about the teacher
every night
high
on
the dog

get
angry
dress
dressed
read
ready

have
a baby
a cold
cold
enough time
sunny

look
after the baby
different
for the money
the money
timetable

New words ▸ *pp. 16–17*

Ist er Engländer? – Nein. **Eigentlich** ist er Waliser.	Is he English? – No. He's Welsh _____ .
Das große Gebäude da drüben ist eine **Moschee**.	The big building over there is a _____ .
Es ist ein ganz **besonderer** Ort.	It's a very _____ place.
Was ist das Besondere an diesem Stadtteil?	_____ this part of town?
Wo kann ich die **Synagoge** finden?	Where can I find the _____ ?
Wir hatten ein gutes **Essen** in diesem Restaurant.	We had a good _____ in that restaurant.
Gibt es dort nur **milde** Gerichte?	Have they only got _____ dishes there?
Oder gibt es auch **scharf gewürzte** Gerichte?	Or have they got _____ dishes too?
Ich liebe Schokolade mit **Nüssen**.	I love chocolate with _____ .
Ich mag Karotten, aber kein anderes **Gemüse**.	I like carrots, but no other _____ .
Kann ich bitte die **Speisekarte** haben?	Can I have the _____ , please?
Die Suppe riecht **seltsam**. Ist sie in Ordnung?	The soup smells _____ . Is it OK?

7 Word search

Finde im Rätsel 16 deutsche Begriffe zum Thema Verkehr.
Schreibe dann das deutsche Wort und die englische Übersetzung auf. (↓ →)

S	T	R	A	S	S	E	N	B	A	H	N
U	D	B	A	H	N	H	O	F	M	U	M
E	I	N	S	T	E	I	G	E	N	M	Q
F	L	U	G	H	A	F	E	N	C	S	A
L	F	A	H	R	R	A	D	H	I	T	U
U	Q	F	L	U	G	Z	E	U	G	E	T
G	Q	T	A	X	I	J	Q	H	F	I	O
S	F	A	H	R	P	L	A	N	A	G	P
T	Z	A	U	S	S	T	E	I	G	E	N
E	Z	T	B	U	S	W	U	E	U	N	E
I	U	F	M	S	F	A	E	H	R	E	K
G	G	B	A	H	N	S	T	E	I	G	T

Straßenbahn – tram

_____

_____

_____

_____

_____

_____

_____

_____

_____

_____

_____

_____

_____

_____

Wenn man Nomen miteinander verbindet, schreibt man sie mal auseinander, mal zusammen.

Eine Regel gibt's leider nicht. Also merkt euch die Einzelfälle!

8 Word building

Verbinde ein Wort aus der Liste mit einem Wort auf den Noten. Trage die deutsche Übersetzung ein.

gear end chair star lessons file hockey room work woman tree bell

1 dancing *lessons* *Tanzstunden*

2 family_____ _____

3 sports_____ _____

4 sound_____ _____

5 ice_____ _____

6 film_____ _____

7 door*bell*_____ _____

8 class_____ _____

9 home_____ _____

10 wheel_____ _____

11 fire_____ _____

12 week_____ _____

9 Odd word out

Ein Wort passt nicht. Finde und unterstreiche es.

1 mosque – synagogue – museum – church

2 giraffe – dinosaur – hippo – rhino

3 recorder – CD player – trombone – flute

4 trendy – sweet – mild – spicy

5 nut – carrot – meal – banana

6 earth – sun – ball – moon

10 The best word

Finde das Wort in der Strickleiter, das am besten in die Lücke passt.

1 Why are you so _____ with me? I haven't done anything wrong.

2 Paul is so _____ . He even finds it hard to say hello to people.

3 Kim felt very _____ when she won the first prize.

4 Rob looked _____ . He didn't understand the joke.

5 Don't be _____ . The dog really isn't dangerous.

6 We were a bit _____ before the test, but it was actually OK.

angry nervous happy shy

alone puzzled lucky shy

angry proud sad sorry

happy puzzled proud scared

alone scared proud sorry

happy lucky nervous sorry

New words ▶ pp. 20–25

Mit dieser **Maschine** kannst du Brot machen.	You can make bread with this _____ .
Seid ihr **zu Fuß** oder mit dem Auto gekommen?	Did you come _____ or by car?
ein Tunnel unter dem **Boden**	a tunnel under the _____
Ich will einen Englisch**kurs** in England machen.	I want do to an English _____ in England.
Was für ein spannender Film!	_____ exciting film!
War diese **Durchsage** für unseren Zug?	Was that _____ for our train?
Wir sind bloß eine normale **Alltags**familie.	We're just a normal _____ family.

11 Hidden words

Ergänze die Wortgruppen, indem du Wörter mit Buchstaben des Wortes „parliament" bildest.

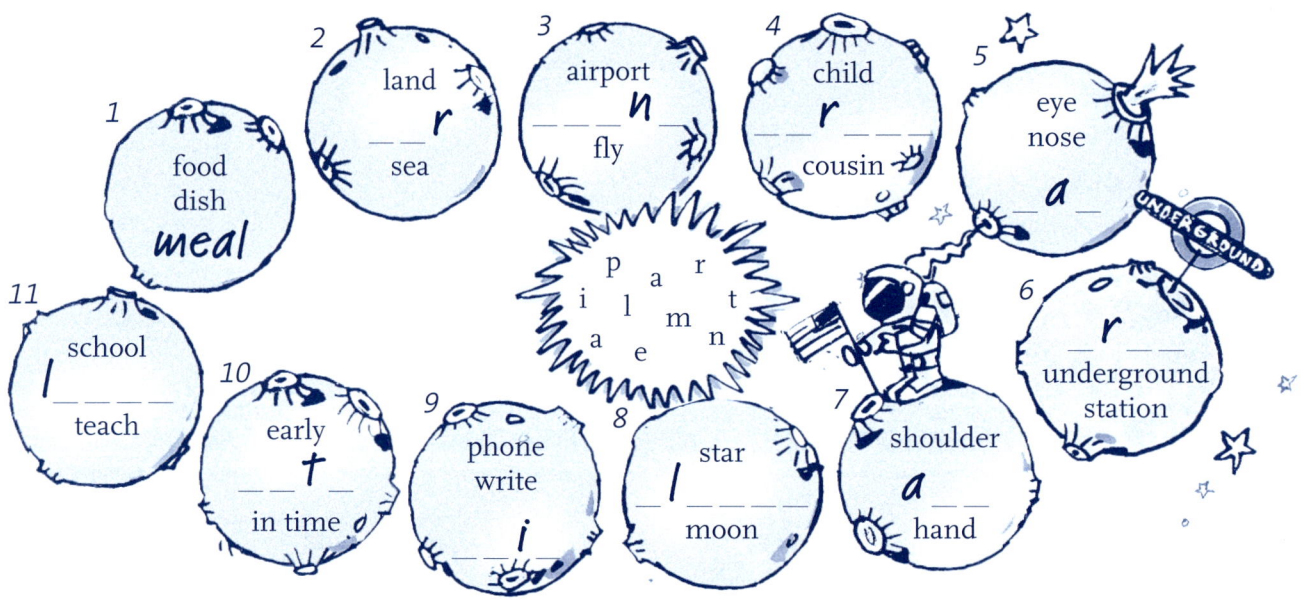

12 Word families

Finde die passenden Verben zu den angegebenen Nomen.

1 dream – *dream*

2 explanation – _____

3 installation – _____

4 winner – _____

5 smile – _____

6 flight – _____

7 actor – _____

8 laughter – _____

9 building – _____

10 description – _____

11 rehearsal – _____

12 glue – _____

13 movement – _____

14 presentation – _____

New words ▸ p. 26

Wie **funktioniert** diese Maschine?	How does this machine _____ ?
Es ist sicherer, einen **Helm** zu tragen.	It's safer to wear a _____ .
Er war **überrascht**, als ich plötzlich hineinkam.	He was _____ when I suddenly came in.
Schnee im Juni – das war sehr **überraschend**!	Snow in June – that was very _____ !
Sag kein Wort! Wir wollen Vati **überraschen**.	Don't say a word! We want to _____ Dad.
Dürfen wir den Raum verlassen?	_____ we _____ to leave the room?
Was steht auf dem **Schild**?	What does the _____ say?
Drück auf den **Knopf** und die Tür wird aufgehen.	Push the _____ and the door will open.
Vor einem Flug bin ich immer **aufgeregt**.	I'm always _____ before a flight.
Es ist **irgendwie** cool, in den Urlaub zu fliegen.	It's _____ cool to fly on holiday.
einen Bericht über einen **Mord** lesen	read a report on a _____
Keiner weiß, wer die Frau **ermordet** hat.	Nobody knows who _____ the woman.
Werden sie den **Mörder** fangen?	Will they catch the _____ ?

13 Pronunciation

Ordne die Wörter aus der Box der richtigen Aussprachegruppe zu.

> Wenn ihr mal Probleme mit der Aussprache habt, hilft die Lautschrift im Dictionary!

already beach beard bread breakfast cheap
clean clear dead dear disappear ear
eastbound head idea leave meant tea

e	iː	ɪə
already	clean	dear
_____	_____	_____
_____	_____	_____
_____	_____	_____
_____	_____	_____

New words ▶ pp. 27–29

Können wir den Unfall**opfern** helfen?	Can we help the _____ of the accident?
Ist das **Blut** oder Ketchup auf deinem Hemd?	Is that _____ or ketchup on your shirt?
Wir haben schöne **Blumen** im Garten.	We've got beautiful _____ in the garden.
Dieser Plan ist nicht sehr **realistisch**.	This plan isn't very _____ .
Zieh bitte den **Stecker** nicht heraus.	Please don't pull out the _____ .
Ohne **Strom** funktioniert kein Computer.	No computer works without _____ .
ein **Lichtblitz** am Himmel	a _____ in the sky
Der Baum warf einen **Schatten** auf das Feld.	The tree threw a _____ on the field.
nahe am Meer, und nicht weit von London	_____ the sea, and not far from London
Er ging weg, **erschien** aber bald wieder.	He went away, but soon _____ again.
Er hatte ein gefährliches **Messer** in der Hand.	He had a dangerous _____ in his hand.
Es ist dunkel! Schalt das **Licht** bitte ein.	It's dark. Please turn on the _____ .
Ich weiß nicht mehr, **was wir tun sollen**.	I don't know _____ .
die **Pfeife** benutzen, um nach Hilfe zu rufen	use the _____ to call for help
Die Geschichte hatte ein unglückliches **Ende**.	The story had an unhappy _____ .
meiner Ansicht nach ...	_____ ...
Wie komme ich voran?	_____ ?
Wir wohnen in einer ruhigen **Gegend**.	We live in a quiet _____ .
Fakten und Daten sind in Geschichte wichtig	_____ and dates are important in history.

14 Opposites

Trage die Gegenteile der fett gedruckten Wörter in die Lücken ein.

1 an **international** / a _national_ festival

2 Do you like **mild** / _____ dishes?

3 This room is very **dirty** / _____ .

4 Turn **left** / _____ at the next corner.

5 a story with a good **beginning** / _____

6 It's **possible** / _____ to get there by bus.

7 Are you planning to **arrive** / _____ early?

8 Only **poor** / _____ people live in this street.

9 Is the supermarket **open** / _____ ?

10 buy a **return** / _____ ticket

15 Hour glasses

Übersetze die Wörter und trage sie in die passende Sanduhr ein.

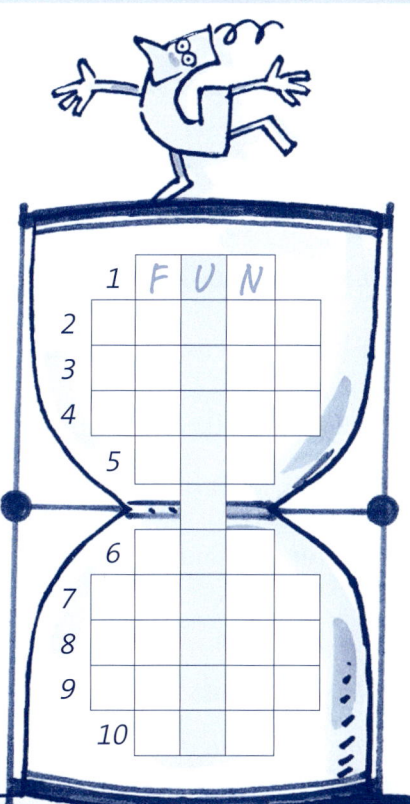

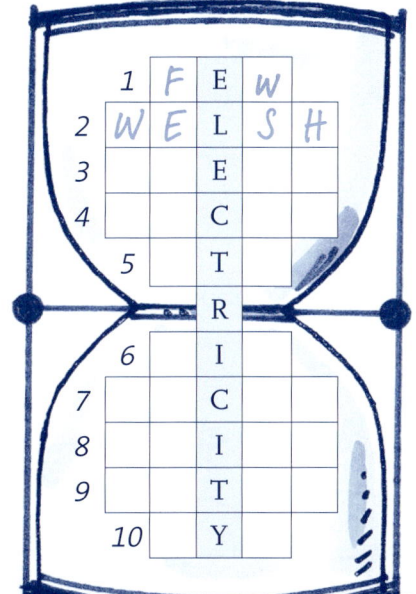

Left hourglass:
- 1 F E W
- 2 W E L S H
- 3 · · E
- 4 · · C
- 5 · · T
- 6 · R
- 7 · I
- 8 · C
- 9 · I · T
- 10 · Y

Right hourglass:
- 1 F U N
- 2
- 3
- 4
- 5
- 6
- 7
- 8
- 9
- 10

1 ein paar/einige – Spaß

2 Geld – walisisch

3 heute – sauber

4 Feind – Tatsachen

5 aß – Arm

6 Mülltonne – Kunst

7 Rauch – Schinkenspeck

8 Rock – Flöte

9 nachdem – sonnig

10 hinzufügen – Auge

Die geheime Wort in der rechten Sanduhr heißt: Englisch _____

Deutsch _____

16 Picture puzzle

Vergleiche die beiden Bilder miteinander. Welche 8 Gegenstände fehlen auf dem rechten Bild?

a firework _____   _____

_____   _____

_____   _____

Unit 2

New words ▶ p. 30

Ein **Lachs** ist ein großer Fisch.	A _____ is a large fish.
Wir brauchen etwas **Öl** für unseren Salat.	We need some _____ for our salad.
eine **riesige** Party mit über 250 Gästen	a _____ party with more than 250 guests
Um die Insel herum liegen viele **Felsen**.	There are lots of _____ around the island.
Der **Bauer** verkaufte sein Gemüse auf dem Markt.	The _____ sold his vegetables at the market.

1 Word friends

Welche Wörter aus den Kieselsteinen passen in die Lücken?

listen · wait · become · eat · do · know · speak · dream · read · keep

1 _eat___ salmon /a huge meal /too much

2 _____ for a bus / for ages / outside

3 _____ on! / of the future / that you can fly

4 _____ a good book /and write / instructions

5 _____ two languages / more slowly / to me

6 _____ to the radio /for the doorbell

7 _____ all the answers / lots of people

8 _____ crosswords / your homework / judo

9 _____ a teacher / tired /very excited

10 _____ in touch / the window open

2 Words with different meanings

Finde in der Liste die passenden Wörter zu den Paaren 1–7.
Trage sie ein und unterstreiche die deutschen Entsprechungen.

3
a) Die Speisekarte liegt auf dem Tisch.
b) Klicke mit der Maus auf das Menü.
_____

2
a) Vergiss nicht das Wechselgeld.
b) Wo müssen wir umsteigen?

a) Ist er ledig oder verheiratet?
b) eine einfache Fahrkarte kaufen

single

1
_____

5
a) Meine Eltern arbeiten in einer Fabrik.
b) Die Fahrstühle waren kaputt, aber jetzt funktionieren sie wieder.
_____

4
a) Das Gegenteil von groß ist klein.
b) Gegenüber dem Kino gibt es ein Café.
_____

change
grow
menu
opposite
single
work
walk

a) schneller wachsen
b) Äpfel anbauen

6
_____

7
a) Lass uns zu Fuß gehen!
b) einen Spaziergang machen
_____

New words ▸ p. 32

Meine Eltern mögen keine **elektronische** Musik.	My parents don't like _____ music.
die neuen **Medien** wie das Internet oder E-Mail	the new _____ like the internet or e-mail
Er hatte keine Freunde und fühlte sich **einsam**.	He had no friends and felt _____ .
Mein **Urgroßvater** wird dieses Jahr 90 Jahre alt.	My _____ will be 90 this year.
Ich hatte nicht viel **Post** – nur einen Brief.	I didn't have much _____ – only one letter.
Ich sah ihn nur **einmal** – oder war es **zweimal**?	I only saw him _____ – or was it _____ ?
Stell dir vor, du bist eine Katze.	_____ you're a cat.
Ich habe eine wichtige **Nachricht** für dich.	I've got important _____ for you.
Schick mir eine **SMS**.	Send me a _____ .
Kannst du mir die Nummer **per SMS schicken**?	Can you _____ me the number?
Rob und ich sind immer gute **Kumpel** gewesen.	Rob and I have always been good _____ .
Es ist **persönlich**. Ich möchte nicht darüber reden.	It's _____ . I don't want to talk about it.
Ich habe einen neuen **Klingelton** für mein Handy.	I've got a new _____ for my mobile.
Wir können diese zwei Lieder **mischen**.	We can _____ these two songs.

3 Number crossword

Gleiche Zahlen sind gleiche Buchstaben.
Die angegebenen Lösungen helfen dir,
das gesamte Rätsel zu lösen.
Alle Wörter sind in dieser Unit neu.

Wo im Rätsel findet man das englische Wort für ...

mischen	*9 across*
riesig	*i down*
zweimal	_____
einsam	_____
Medien	_____
Kumpel	_____
sich (etwas) vorstellen	_____
Nachbarn	_____

New words ▸ *p. 33*

Wie lange **dauert** der Flug nach Berlin?

How long does the flight to Berlin _____ ?

Ich kann dich am Flughafen **abholen**.

I can _____ you _____ at the airport.

Informationen aus einem **Fahrplan** bekommen

get information from a _____

Die **Ankunft**szeit ist jeden Tag dieselbe.

The _____ time is the same every day.

Kannst du mir die **Abfahrt**szeit sagen?

Can you tell me the _____ time?

Er kam früh und blieb **bis** 13 Uhr.

He came early and stayed _____ 1 pm.

Der Laden ist geöffnet **von** Montag **bis** Sonnabend.

The shop opens _____ Monday _____ Saturday.

4 Scrambled words: school

Löse die Buchstabenrätsel, um Wörter zu finden, die mit Schule zusammenhängen.
Trage die deutschen Übersetzungen ein. Die markierten Buchstaben ergeben das „geheime Wort".

1 Teal Bit Em   T I M E T A B L E   *Stundenplan*

2 Trace Eh   __ __ __ __ __ __ __

3 Cam Tassel   __ __ __ __ __ __ __ __

4 Hay Idols   __ __ __ __ __ __ __ __

5 Bad Or   __ __ __ __ __ __

6 Sic Enec   __ __ __ __ __ __ __

7 Carom Loss   __ __ __ __ __ __ __ __ __ __

5 Last letter – first letter

Der letzte Buchstabe von jedem Wort ist
gleichzeitig der erste des nächsten Wortes.

1 Fahrplan
2 aufgeregt
3 Abfahrt
4 Elefant
5 dauern/(Zeit)
   brauchen
6 Aufzug
7 Fels
8 Schlüssel
9 du/ihr/dir/euch
10 bis
11 einsam
12 gähnen

6 Word groups

Übersetze die deutschen Wörter in der Box ins Englische und füge sie in die richtige Wortgruppe ein.

farm animals	media	public transport
chicken		

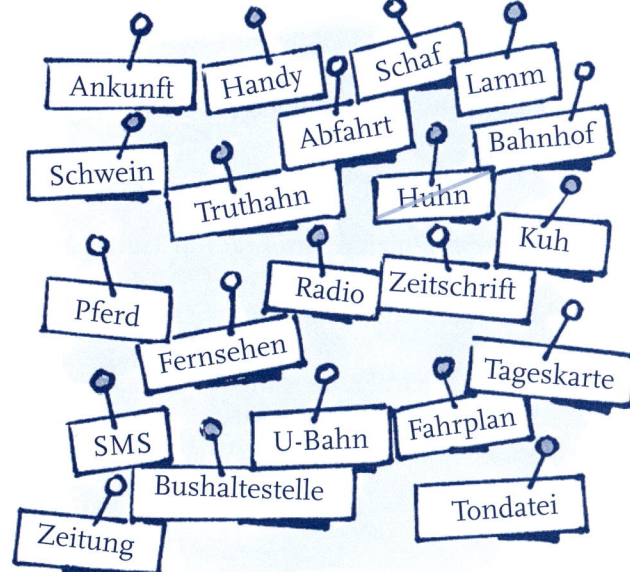

Ankunft · Handy · Schaf · Lamm · Abfahrt · Bahnhof · Schwein · Truthahn · Huhn · Kuh · Pferd · Radio · Zeitschrift · Fernsehen · Tageskarte · SMS · U-Bahn · Fahrplan · Bushaltestelle · Tondatei · Zeitung

7 Making phrases

Vervollständige die Audrücke mit dem Verb vom richtigen Zettel.

1 *take* _____ a photo of the cows in the field

2 _____ a text message to a friend

3 _____ the arrival times in the timetable

4 _____ all the hungry farm animals

5 _____ the train at the next station

6 _____ your mum on your mobile

7 _____ at the bus stop

8 _____ a sound file from the internet

take · download · wait · phone · check · get off · feed · send

8 Spot the mistakes

In jedem Satz sind zwei Fehler. Unterstreiche und korrigiere sie. Es gibt Rechtschreib- und grammatische Fehler.

1 Hoy is one of the <u>biger</u> Orkney ilands.　　*bigger*　_____

2 Live on an island can be lonly sometimes.　_____　_____

3 Katrina have a mobil, so she often texts her friends.　_____　_____

4 She also write e-mails once or twice a weak.　_____　_____

5 She sometimes downloads musik from a webseite.　_____　_____

6 Last weekend she taked lots of fotos at the ceilidh.　_____　_____

New words ▸ *p. 34*

Ich mag ihn – er ist ein freundlicher **Typ**.	I like him – he's a friendly _____ .
Sein erster Tag im neuen Job ist **gut verlaufen**.	His first day in the new job _____ .
Ich **kann** mit dieser Brille besser sehen.	I'm _____ see better with these glasses.
Wir mussten einen großen **Rucksack** packen.	We had to pack a big _____ .
Ich kann nicht weggehen – ich **erwarte** Besucher.	I can't go out – I'm _____ visitors.
Ich hatte kein Essen – **nicht einmal** ein Stück Brot.	I had no food – _____ a piece of bread.
Ihre Haare sind zu kurz für einen **Pferdeschwanz**.	Her hair is too short for a _____ .

9 What are the words?

*Welches Wort passt besser in
die Lücken:* **able** *oder* **allowed**?

Denkt daran:
able to benutzt man,
wenns eher um das
Können geht ...

... *und*
wenns um
das Dürfen geht,
benutzt man
allowed to.

1 Mum! Look at the sign. You **aren't** ___*allowed*___ to leave the car here.

2 The homework was so difficult. Even Dad **wasn't** _____ **to** help me with it.

3 Dilek's very good at languages. She's _____ **to** speak German, Turkish and English.

4 **Are** we _____ **to** cycle in the park? – No, we aren't. The sign says 'No bikes'.

5 Sorry, I won't **be** _____ **to** meet you later. I just haven't got enough time.

6 I'm _____ **to** stay up late at weekends, but I have to go to bed at 9 on weekdays.

10 Word pairs

Welche Wörter passen zusammen?

eat

course
helmet
light
meal
menu
message
suitcase
trombone

wear

send

play

message   pack

do

read

turn off

New words ▸ p. 35

Ich bin **gekränkt**, weil du unhöflich zu mir warst.	I'm _____ because you were rude to me.
Es **kränkt** mich, wenn du unhöflich bist.	It _____ me when you're rude.
die **Schönheit** der Berge Schottlands	the _____ of Scotland's mountains
Er **hat** mir wieder **Schimpfwörter nachgerufen**.	He _____ me _____ again.
Mutti **erlaubt** mir nicht, Make-up zu tragen.	Mum doesn't _____ me wear make-up.
Ich **würde** mich auf einer Insel einsam fühlen.	I _____ feel lonely on an island.
Entschuldigung. Das war ein **dummer** Fehler.	Sorry. That was a _____ mistake.
Leider gibt's an jeder Schule einen **Schultyrannen**.	I'm afraid there's a _____ at every school.
Vergiss nicht abzuschließen, wenn du gehst.	Don't _____ to lock up when you go.
Sei nicht so aufgeregt. Entspann dich **einfach**!	Don't be so nervous. _____ relax!
Ich wollte nicht deine **Gefühle verletzen**.	I didn't want to hurt your _____ .
im Wörterbuch nach dem **Eintrag** suchen	look for the _____ in the dictionary
Sein Name steht **über** seiner Adresse und	His name is _____ the address and
... seine Telefonnummer ist **unter** der Adresse.	... his telephone number is below the address.
Was ist die **Übersetzung** dieses Wortes?	What's the _____ of this word?
Kannst du dieses Wort ins Deutsche **übersetzen**?	Can you _____ this word into German?
Nein, aber ich kann die **Bedeutung** erraten.	No, but I can guess the _____ .
eine falsche Antwort und eine **korrekte** Antwort	a wrong answer and a _____ answer

11 Lost words

Die fehlenden Wörter stecken im Maul des Hais.
Finde sie und ergänze die Sätze.

1 The water here can be dangerous, so it's _unsafe_ to go swimming.

2 It's _____ to eat fruit and vegetables every day.

3 Jane's room is always in a mess – she's so _____ !

4 I think it's _____ if you don't do any sport.

5 Sue never laughs or smiles. She can't be a very _____ person.

6 Tim never says hello to anyone. Why is he so _____ ?

tidy
happy
healthy
unhappy
unsafe
untidy
unhealthy
safe
unfriendly

New words ▸ *pp. 38-42*

Die **Betonung** liegt auf der dritten Silbe.	The _____ is on the third syllable.
Dein Aufsatz braucht eine bessere **Gliederung**.	Your essay needs a better _____ .
Ich heiße Daniel. Ich **werde** auch Dan **genannt**.	My name's Daniel. I, ___ also _____ Dan.
Bist du sicher, dass diese **Aussage** korrekt ist?	Are you sure this _____ is correct?
eine **Rolle** in einem berühmten Film spielen	play a _____ in a famous film
Millionen Menschen sahen diesen Film.	_____ of people saw this film.
Der See ist 14 **Kilometer** lang.	The lake is 14 _____ long.
Wieviele **Zentimeter** hat ein Meter?	How many _____ are there in a metre?

12 Word search: town and country

Im Rätsel sind 18 „town and country"-Wörter versteckt.
Finde sie und übersetze sie ins Deutsche. (↓ →)

H	H	A	R	B	O	U	R	V	P	B	S
I	T	O	W	E	R	F	S	F	A	R	M
L	D	S	Q	U	A	R	E	K	F	N	C
L	Y	E	Z	C	E	Z	A	R	W	P	R
B	M	L	A	A	B	I	S	L	A	N	D
E	O	A	W	N	R	O	A	D	T	Y	G
A	U	K	J	A	I	T	N	Y	G	I	H
C	N	E	F	L	D	U	Z	Y	Y	W	G
H	T	R	H	M	G	F	I	E	L	D	R
C	A	S	T	L	E	H	C	O	A	S	T
O	I	J	S	T	A	T	I	O	N	C	R
D	N	Z	O	D	R	B	A	Y	S	L	K

sea	Meer
_____	_____
_____	_____
_____	_____
_____	_____
_____	_____
_____	_____
_____	_____
_____	_____
_____	_____
_____	_____
_____	_____
_____	_____
_____	_____

13 More about ... Orkney

Vervollständige den Text mit Wörtern vom Ticket.

another
between
biggest
but
fewest
for
history
islands
make
on
takes
under

ORKNEY TICKET

Orkney is a group of _islands_ (1) ten miles from the Scottish coast. Today, about

20,000 people live _____ (2) 17 of the 70 islands. Most – about 15,000 – live on the

_____ (3) island, Mainland. Between five _____ (4) 550 people live on the

other islands. Hoy, the second largest island, has just under 300 people.

Orkney hasn't got many people, _____ (5) it has lots of schools – 21 for about 3,300

students. Some of the schools are very small – four of them have

_____ (6) ten students.

When people travel from one island to _____ (7) they go by

ferry, or fly between the bigger islands. The shortest flight is

_____ (8) Westray and Papa Westray – it _____ (9)

only two minutes.

Orkney is great _____ (10) holidays. If you go there, you can

stay on a farm and learn how to _____ (11) cheese, enjoy the

clean air and beautiful beaches and find out more about the 5,500

year _____ (12) of the people on the islands.

14 The best word

Finde das Wort in der Strickleiter, das am besten in die Lücke passt.

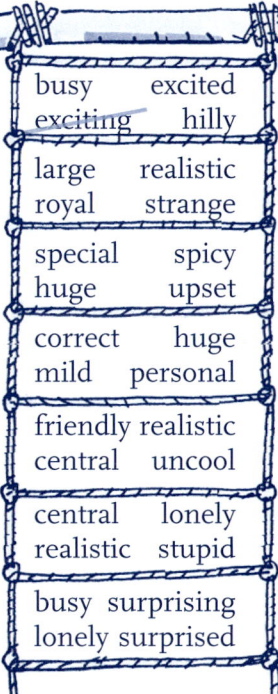

| busy | excited |
| exciting | hilly |

| large | realistic |
| royal | strange |

| special | spicy |
| huge | upset |

| correct | huge |
| mild | personal |

| friendly | realistic |
| central | uncool |

| central | lonely |
| realistic | stupid |

| busy | surprising |
| lonely | surprised |

1 Here's some _exciting_ news. Mum's going to have another baby!

2 Open a window please. There's a _____ smell in the room.

3 Kim was very _____ because nobody came to visit her.

4 They live in a _____ house with 17 bedrooms.

5 Nobody likes Angela. She's so _____ !

6 Fantastic! That's a very _____ plan.

7 I was _____ when I saw Peter. I thought he was abroad.

New words ▸ *pp. 44–47*

Schönes Lied! Lass mich es **noch einmal** hören.	Nice song! Let me hear it _____ .
Möchtest du **eine Tasse** Tee?	Would you like a _____ ?
In Großbritannien fährt **man** links.	In Great Britain _____ drive on the left.
Ein Vogel **prallte gegen die Windschutzscheibe**.	A bird _____ .
Die **Schulversammlung** begann um 8.50.	_____ started at 8.50.
Der **Schulleiter** machte eine Ankündigung.	The _____ made an announcement.
Das kann nicht wahr sein – ich **glaube** es nicht.	That can't be true – I don't _____ it.
Es **könnte vielleicht** regnen – hast du eine Jacke?	It _____ rain – have you got a jacket?
Wenn es regnet, **könnten** wir ins Museum gehen.	If it rains, we _____ go to the museum.
Welcher **Friseur schneidet** dir die Haare?	Which _____ your hair?
Der Wind **blies** vom Westen.	The wind _____ from the west.
Er rannte schnell über die Straße **hinüber**.	He ran quickly _____ the road.
Dieser **Anorak** ist schön warm.	This _____ is nice and warm.
Der Film **beginnt** um 8 und ist um 10 Uhr vorbei.	The film _____ at 8 and is over at 10 o'clock.
Das Schaf Dolly war ein berühmter **Klon**.	The sheep Dolly was a famous _____ .
Ist er **neidisch auf** meinen neuen Computer?	Is he _____ my new computer?
Ich brauche Fleisch und Gemüse für den **Eintopf**.	I need meat and vegetables for the _____ .
Die meisten Dörfer haben eine **Gemeindehalle**.	Most villages have a _____ .
Der Dieb **schnappte** mein Handy und rannte weg.	The thief _____ my mobile and ran away.
ein Wort im Wörterbuch **nachschlagen**	_____ a word in the dictionary

15 The fourth word

Welchers Wort fehlt hier?

1 one – two	once – _____	*5* good – bad	intelligent – _____
2 can – may	able to – _____	*6* ride – ridden	forget – _____
3 come – arrival	go – _____	*7* over – under	above – _____
4 build – building	feel – _____	*8* invite – invitation	translate – _____

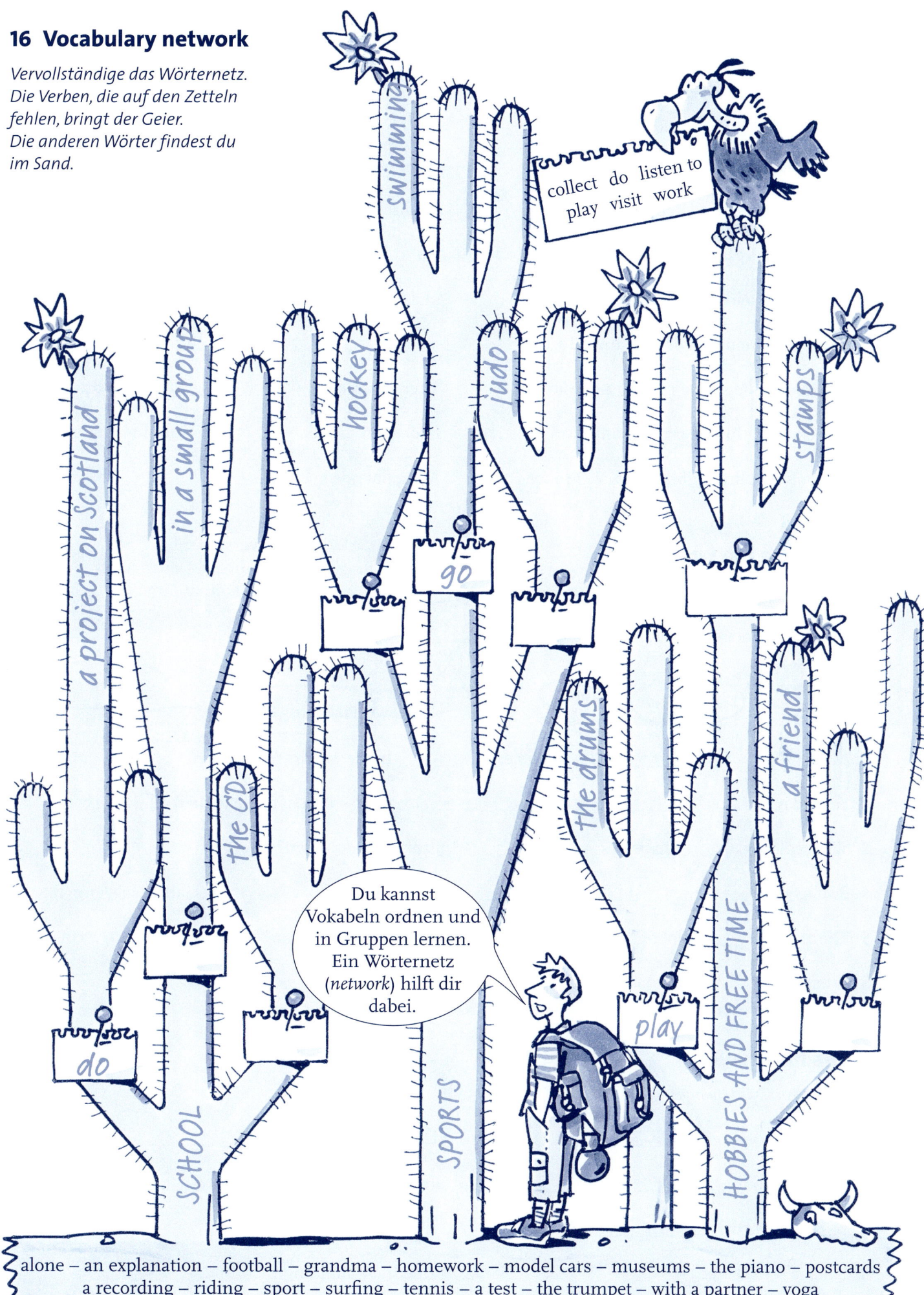

16 Vocabulary network

Vervollständige das Wörternetz.
Die Verben, die auf den Zetteln
fehlen, bringt der Geier.
Die anderen Wörter findest du
im Sand.

collect   do   listen to
play   visit   work

swimming

hockey   ludo   stamps

a project on Scotland   in a small group

go

the CD   the drums   a friend

do   play

Du kannst
Vokabeln ordnen und
in Gruppen lernen.
Ein Wörternetz
(*network*) hilft dir
dabei.

SCHOOL   SPORTS   HOBBIES AND FREE TIME

alone – an explanation – football – grandma – homework – model cars – museums – the piano – postcards
a recording – riding – sport – surfing – tennis – a test – the trumpet – with a partner – yoga

Unit 3

New words ▶ pp. 52–53

Hast du wirklich Karten für das **Endspiel**?	Have you really got tickets for the _____ ?
Leider wird dies sein **letztes** Spiel sein.	I'm afraid this will be his _____ game.
Er gewann das **Halbfinale**, verlor aber das Endspiel.	He won the _____ , but lost the final.
eine **Trainingseinheit** verpassen	miss a _____
Ich **interessiere mich für** Judo und Hockey.	_____ judo and hockey.
Auf dem Bett liegt eine rote **Tagesdecke**.	There's a red _____ on the bed.
Versteck dich hinter dem **Vorhang** am Fenster!	Hide behind the _____ in the window!
Eine große Wohnung braucht viele **Möbel**.	A big flat needs lots of _____ .

1 What are the words?

Finde für jeden Satz ein passendes deutsches Wort. Übersetze es und setze es ein. Wähle dann die richtige Form des Verbs **be**.

Nicht vergessen! Es gibt Wörter, die im Deutschen Plural sein können, im Englischen aber immer Einzahl sind.

Verkehrsmittel   Nachrichten   Möbel   Hausaufgaben   Haare   Informationen

1 All the _*information*_ about Manchester __*is*__ in the brochure. (is/are)

2 Yesterday's Maths _____ _____ so hard – I wasn't able to do it all. (were/was)

3 What colour _____ Latisha's _____ ? Black or dark brown? (are/is)

4 Public _____ here _____ very good. The buses are always late. (isn't/aren't)

5 There _____ a lot of _____ in the room – only a few chairs. (weren't/wasn't)

6 What time _____ the next _____ on TV? (is/are)

2 The fourth word

Welches Wort wird hier gesucht?

1 two – one / twice – _*once*_

2 plane – airport / ship – _____

3 pig – pork / cow – _____

4 banana – fruit / pea – _____

5 afraid – of / interested – _____

6 bread – food / armchair – _____

7 rain – fall / wind – _____

8 cathedral – building / trumpet – _____

3 Hidden words

Ergänze die Wortgruppen, indem du Wörter mit Buchstaben der Wörter „training session" bildest.

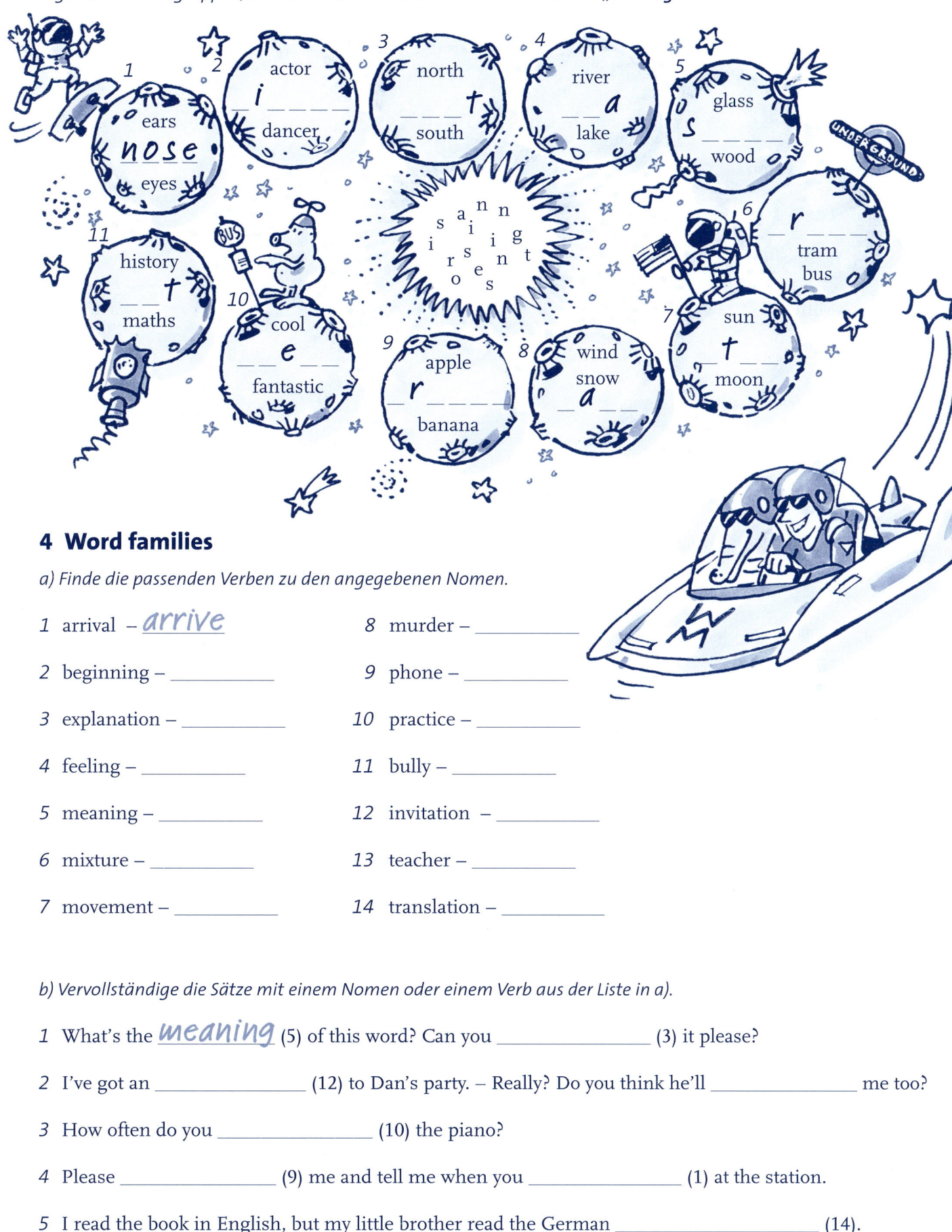

1 ears
nose
eyes

2 actor
_ _ _ _ i _
dancer

3 north
_ _ _ _ t
south

4 river
_ _ _ a
lake

5 glass
s _ _ _ _ _
wood

6 _ _ r _ _ _ _
tram
bus

7 sun
_ _ t _ _ _
moon

8 wind
snow
_ _ a _ _

9 apple
r _ _ _ _ _
banana

10 cool
_ _ _ e _ _ _
fantastic

11 history
_ _ _ t _
maths

s a n n
i i g
r s n t
o e
s

4 Word families

a) Finde die passenden Verben zu den angegebenen Nomen.

1 arrival – *arrive*

2 beginning – _____

3 explanation – _____

4 feeling – _____

5 meaning – _____

6 mixture – _____

7 movement – _____

8 murder – _____

9 phone – _____

10 practice – _____

11 bully – _____

12 invitation – _____

13 teacher – _____

14 translation – _____

b) Vervollständige die Sätze mit einem Nomen oder einem Verb aus der Liste in a).

1 What's the *meaning* (5) of this word? Can you _____ (3) it please?

2 I've got an _____ (12) to Dan's party. – Really? Do you think he'll _____ me too?

3 How often do you _____ (10) the piano?

4 Please _____ (9) me and tell me when you _____ (1) at the station.

5 I read the book in English, but my little brother read the German _____ (14).

New words ▸ pp. 54–55

In unserem Verein **trainieren** wir jeden Montag.	In our club we _____ every Monday.
Unsere **Anhänger** kommen zu jedem Spiel.	Our _____ come to every match.
Viele Jugendliche **unterstützen** die Mannschaft.	Lots of teenagers _____ the team.
Versuch mal, den neuen Spieler zu **entdecken**.	Try and _____ the new player.
Ein **Unentschieden** hilft uns nicht.	A _____ won't help us.
Das Spiel endete 2 **beide**.	The game ended _____ .
Warum hat Smith kein **Tor geschossen**?	Why didn't Smith _____ ?
Nach 45 Minuten war der **Spielstand** 2:1.	After 45 minutes the _____ was 2:1
Die Fans jubelten, als Black ein **Tor** schoss.	The fans cheered when Black scored a _____ .
Ist der **Trainer** böse auf seine Spieler?	Is the _____ angry with his players?
Die **Atmosphäre** beim Spiel war toll.	The _____ at the match was great.
Dein neuer **Gymnastikanzug** sieht sehr schön aus!	Your new _____ looks great!
Passt die blaue **Strumpfhose** zu roten Schuhen?	Do the blue _____ go with red shoes.
ein deutscher **Austauschschüler** in England	a German _____ in England
Klopfe, bevor du den Raum **betrittst**!	Knock before you _____ the room!
Ich war nicht da, als er kam. – **Schlechtes Timing**!	I was out when he came. – _____ !
Hungrig? – Nein, ich habe keinen **Appetit**.	Hungry? – No, I've got no _____ .
Die Fragen **beziehen** sich **auf** Seite 3.	The questions _____ page 3.

5 Word friends

In jedem Haus gibt es drei Wörter bzw. Wortverbindungen, die man direkt nach dem Verb auf der Fahne benutzen kann. Unterstreiche sie.

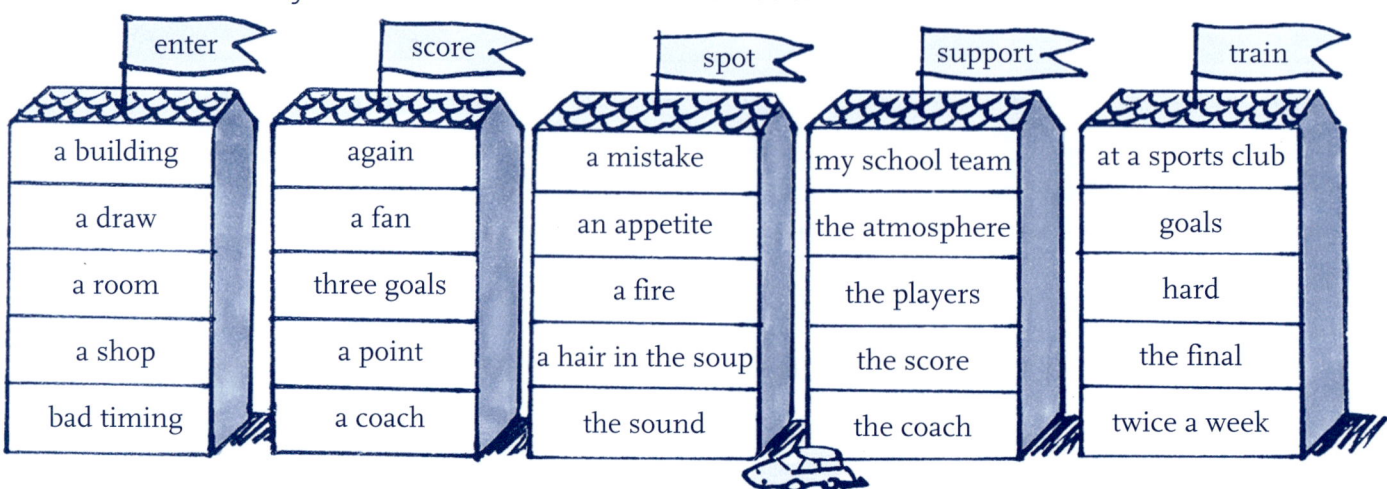

enter	score	spot	support	train
a building	again	a mistake	my school team	at a sports club
a draw	a fan	an appetite	the atmosphere	goals
a room	three goals	a fire	the players	hard
a shop	a point	a hair in the soup	the score	the final
bad timing	a coach	the sound	the coach	twice a week

6 Words in pictures

a) *Trage die angezeigten Körperteile ein.*

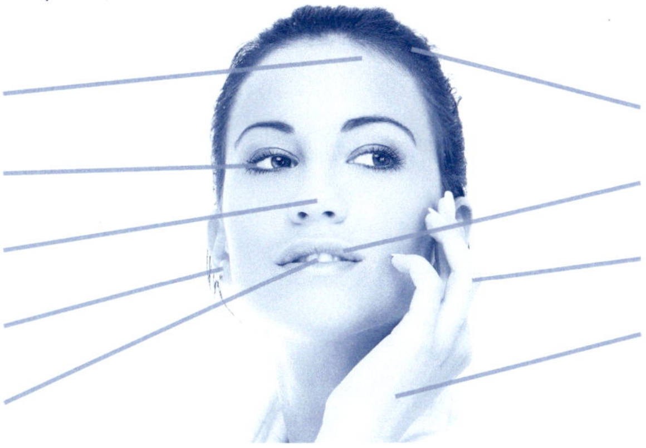

1 _face_
2 _____
3 _____
4 _____
5 _____

6 _____
7 _____
8 _____
9 _____

b) *Unterstreiche die beiden Wörter, die am besten zu den fettgedruckten Wörtern passen.*

1 a broken / pretty / round **face**

2 blue / bright / loud **eyes**

3 a long / small / tidy **nose**

4 my left / medium / right **ear**

5 broken / careful / white **teeth**

6 grey / slow / tidy **hair**

7 a big / early / loud **mouth**

8 cheap / clean / strong **hands**

7 Definitions

Vervollständige die Definitionen mit Wörtern aus den Mauersteinen. Trage die richtigen Wörter aus der Sprühwolke in die rechte Spalte ein.

clone   farmer
final   furniture
hairdresser   head teacher
lonely   supporter

alone   country   hair
looks   last   matches
most   person   pigs   school
sit   sofas   team
washes   winner   unhappy

1 a person who _washes_ and cuts other people's _____   _hairdresser_

2 a person who _____ like a copy of another _____   _____

3 a person who really likes a _____ , wears team colours, goes to _____   _____

4 the _____ match – the _____ is the champion   _____

5 things like chairs or _____ where you can _____ or lie down   _____

6 the _____ important teacher at a _____   _____

7 a person who works in the _____ , often with cows, _____ etc.   _____

8 _____ because you are _____ or have no friends   _____

New words ▸ pp. 56–57

Die **ganze** Familie wird dieses Museum mögen. The _____ family will love this museum.

ein **Künstler**, der Städte malt an _____ who paints cities

Das Spiel beginnt um 20 Uhr im **Stadion**. The match starts at 8 pm in the _____ .

Lass uns eine **Abmachung treffen**! Let's _____ !

versuchen, einen Satz zu **umschreiben** try to _____ a sentence

Ich habe eine **allgemeine** Frage zu Schottland. I have a _____ question about Scotland.

Können wir diese Mannschaft **schlagen**? Can we _____ this team?

einen **Pokal** gewinnen win a _____

Es war ein fantastischer **Sieg** über United. It was a fantastic _____ against United.

Am Ende waren wir die bessere Mannschaft. _____ we were the better team.

Der Spielstand in der **Halbzeit** war 2:1. The score at _____ was 2:1.

Es war ein toller **Schuss**, aber It was a great _____ , but

... der **Torwart** hat den Ball gehalten. ... the _____ held the ball.

8 Word ladder

Gehe von unten nach oben, indem du bei jeder Sprosse einen Buchstaben veränderst.

luck

Good ★ in your English test tomorrow.

Please close the windows and ★ up before you leave.

I can't find my key. Can you help me ★ for it?

prepare hot meals

I ★ some photos with my new camera yesterday.

How many pages are there in that ★ ?

The English word for Fußballschuh is football ★.

You can travel on water with this.

Manchester United ★ Bayern Munich 2:1.

★ from a cow is called beef.

Let's ★ tomorrow at 4 o'clock.

one foot – two ★

give food to an animal or person

need

The show is free, so we don't ★ any tickets.

9 Last letter – first letter

Der letzte Buchstabe von jedem Wort ist gleichzeitig der erste des nächsten Wortes.

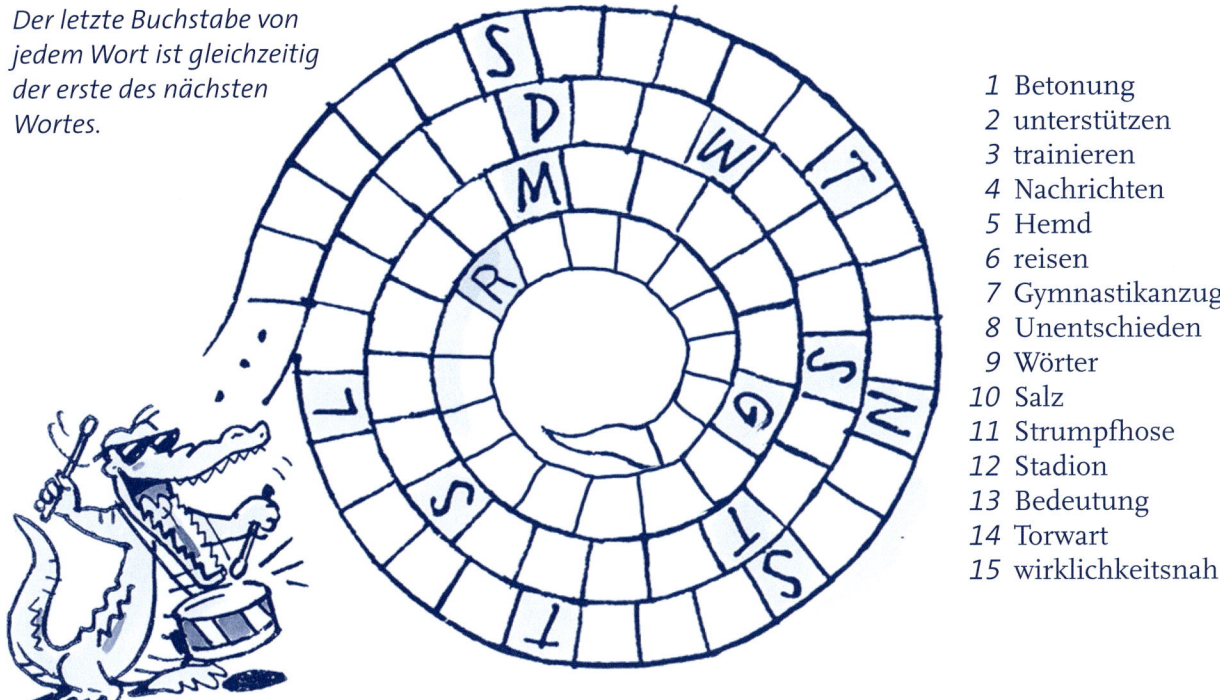

1 Betonung
2 unterstützen
3 trainieren
4 Nachrichten
5 Hemd
6 reisen
7 Gymnastikanzug
8 Unentschieden
9 Wörter
10 Salz
11 Strumpfhose
12 Stadion
13 Bedeutung
14 Torwart
15 wirklichkeitsnah

10 Pronunciation

Ordne die Wörter aus der Box der richtigen Aussprachegruppe zu.

Englische Aussprache ist nicht immer einfach …

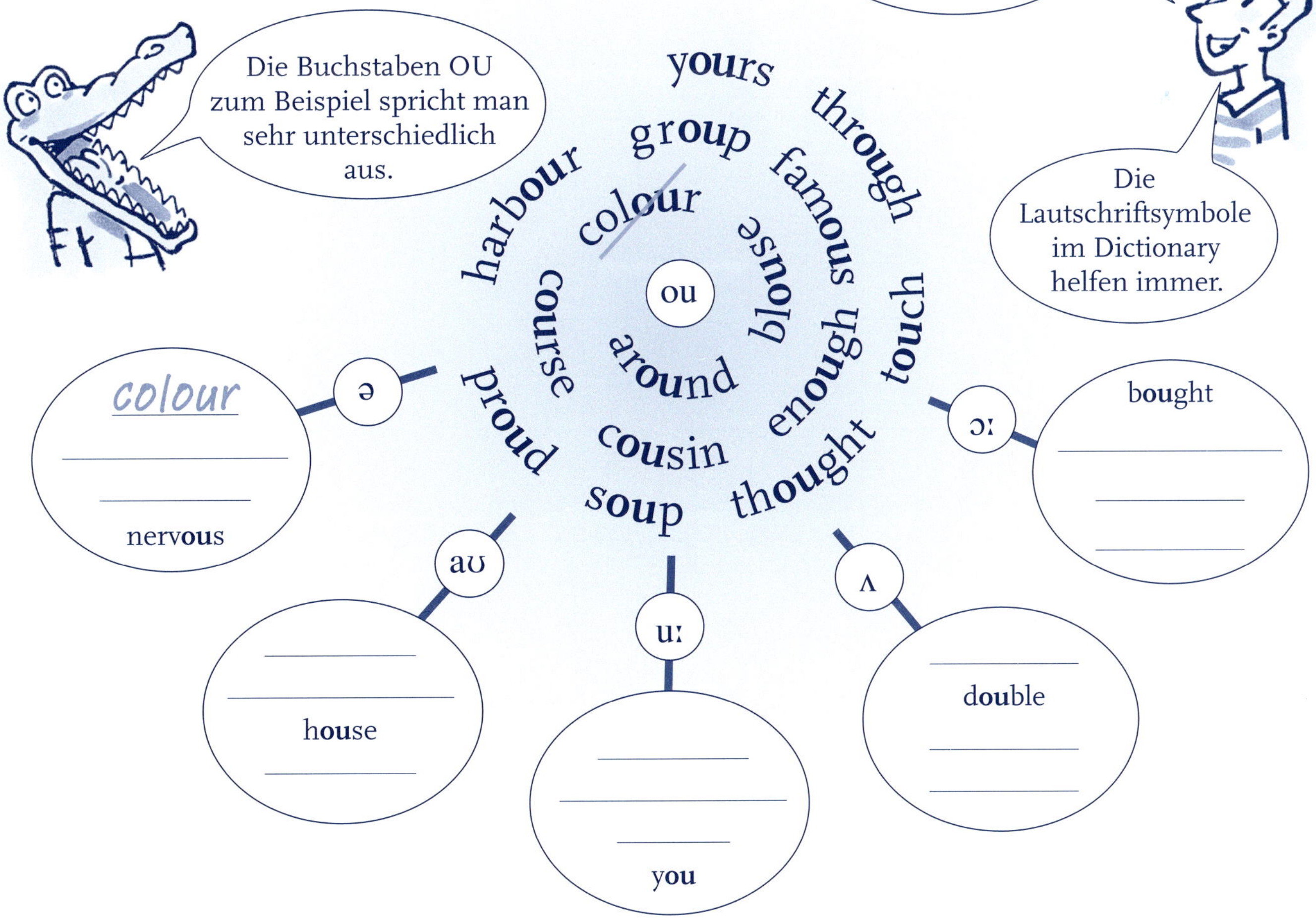

Die Buchstaben OU zum Beispiel spricht man sehr unterschiedlich aus.

Die Lautschriftsymbole im Dictionary helfen immer.

yours
group
through
harbour
colour
famous
course
house
ou
around
blouse
proud
cousin
enough
touch
soup
thought
thought

ə — colour / nervous

aʊ — house

uː — you

ɔː — bought

ʌ — double

New words ▸ *pp. 60–65*

der **Unterschied** zwischen Stadt und Land	the _____ between town and country
Die Suppe braucht noch etwas **Pfeffer**.	The soup needs some more _____ .
Ich meine, die Suppe braucht noch etwas **Salz**.	I think the soup needs some more _____ .
Sätze in die richtige **Reihenfolge** bringen	put sentences into the right _____
Wie **endete** die erste Halbzeit?	How did the first half _____ ?
Schreibe einige Sätze **über dich selbst**.	Write some sentences _____ .

11 Crossword

Across ➡

1 Badehose (8, 6)
5 Laufbahn (7, 5)
7 Spiel (5)
8 Sieg (3)
10 Tor (4)
14 Reitweg (6, 4)
17 Trainer/in (7)
18 Helm (6)
19 Endspiel (5)
21 Anhänger/in, Fan (9)

Down ⬇

1 Schwimm-becken (8, 4)
2 Laufschuhe (7, 5)
3 Stadion (7)
4 Skipiste (3, 5)
6 Mannschaft (4)
9 Halbzeit (4)
11 Sporthalle (5, 4)
12 Sattel (6)
13 Torwart, Torfrau (10)
15 trainieren (5)
16 Spielfeld (5)
20 Pokal (3)

12 More about ... Manchester United

Vervollständige den Text mit den Wörtern aus der Box.

club   even   huge   learn
match   millions   over   rich
players   third   than   times

Manchester United is a famous English football _club_. (1) They've been football champions of England 16 _____ (2) and, in 1968, they were the first English club to win the European Cup. In 2008 they won it a _____ (3) time. ManU isn't just popular in England. All _____ (4) the world, the club has _____ (5) of supporters. And it is very _____ (6), so it has enough money to buy the best _____ (7) (like Wayne Rooney or Cristiano Ronaldo). ManU's home is the _____ (8) stadium at Old Trafford, with room for 75,000 fans to watch a _____ (9). The club has _____ (10) got a museum. More _____ (11) 200,000 visitors go there every year to _____ (12) about ManU's great past.

13 Hour glasses

Übersetze die Wörter und trage sie in die passende Sanduhr ein.

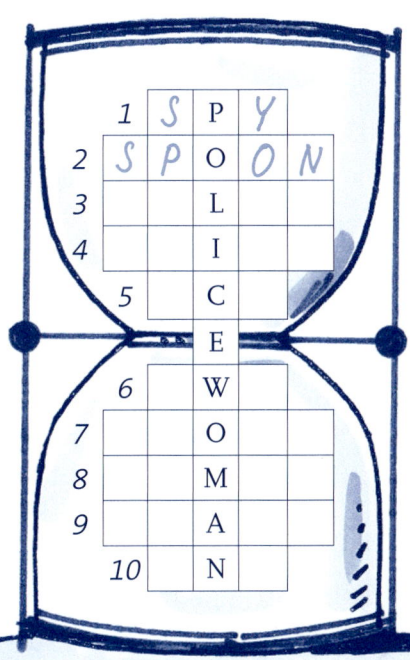

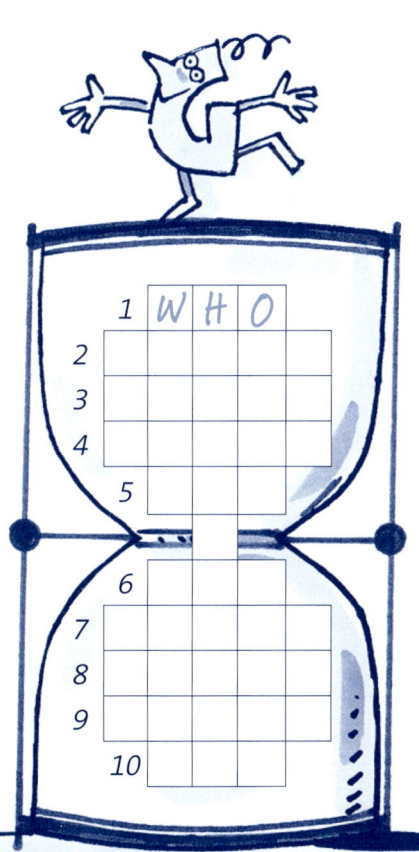

1 wer – Spion
2 Trainer – Löffel
3 Lineal –Preis, Gewinn
4 sich beeilen – Hemd
5 Eis – hinzufügen
6 Kugelschreiber – zwei
7 gekränkt – Spielstand
8 Aufsatz – römisch
9 Stahl – Zug
10 Schluss – Kunst

Left hourglass:
1 S P Y
2 S P O O N
3 . L
4 . I
5 . C
6 E
6 . W
7 . O
8 . M
9 . A
10 N

Right hourglass:
1 W H O

Das geheime Wort heißt: Englisch _____
                            Deutsch _____

New words ▸ p. 66; p. 104

Wir müssen noch nicht gehen – es ist **erst** 8 Uhr.	We don't have to go yet – it's _____ 8 am.
Papa ist in einer großen Familie **aufgewachsen**.	Dad _____ in a big family.
Wenn ich **erwachsen bin**, möchte ich Arzt werden.	When I _____ I'd like to be a doctor.
Jack schob den Rollstuhl **auf** die Fähre.	Jack pushed the wheelchair _____ the ferry.
Lass uns eine Boots**fahrt** auf dem See **machen**.	Let's _____ a boat _____ on the lake.
Ein Unfall! Ruf einen **Krankenwagen**!	An accident! Call an _____!
Bob ist Trainer für **Leichathletik** und Schwimmer.	Bob's an _____ and swimming coach.
Der Sieger bekam eine Gold**medaille**.	The winner got a gold _____.
Kannst du ein Bild von einem Fuchs **zeichnen**?	Can you _____ a picture of a fox?
Die Spieler mussten hart **um** den Titel **kämpfen**.	The players had to _____ hard _____ the title.
Die **Operation** hat ihm das Leben gerettet.	The _____ saved his life.
Sind diese Blumen **künstlich** oder echt?	Are these flowers _____ or real?
Schnee! Nun kann ich meinen **Schlitten** benutzen.	Snow! Now I can use my _____!
ein Spieler mit viel **Talent**	a player with lots of _____
Ich benutze den Rollstuhl, weil ich **behindert** bin.	I use the wheelchair because I'm _____.
Sie gewann eine Medaille bei den **Meisterschaften**.	She won a medal at the _____.
Wie oft hat sie England **vertreten**?	How often did she _____ England?

14 Verb forms

Ergänze die Tabelle der unregelmäßigen Verben.

1	do	did	done		8	begin		
2		grew up			9		blew	
3		took			10			cut
4	draw				11			forgotten
5	fight				12		let	
6			beaten		13	upset		
7		chose			14			caught

15 Word search

Finde Wörter im Rätsel, um die Wortgruppen zu vervollständigen. (↓ →)

G	H	D	S	A	U	S	A	G	E	L	O	C	B	K	R	H	N
O	A	A	P	E	V	O	L	L	E	Y	B	A	L	L	R	E	K
A	M	K	A	S	C	O	U	R	T	J	S	S	O	E	X	L	N
L	B	S	R	A	P	L	A	N	E	F	T	T	U	S	T	I	I
B	U	K	A	L	S	T	A	D	I	U	M	E	S	H	R	C	U
O	R	I	L	A	J	W	G	S	O	C	K	W	E	E	A	O	T
T	G	R	Y	D	Z	B	L	S	G	S	K	I	S	L	M	P	I
R	E	T	M	U	W	Y	B	U	S	J	A	X	F	F	Y	T	G
O	R	S	P	F	U	N	D	E	R	G	R	O	U	N	D	E	H
U	F	O	I	T	M	C	Z	C	S	M	S	G	R	A	U	R	T
S	S	U	C	T	E	M	X	H	O	W	Q	P	N	T	W	P	S
E	H	P	S	A	D	S	R	I	F	K	X	C	I	H	A	G	V
R	O	Q	B	D	A	H	W	P	A	F	T	H	T	L	R	Z	F
S	R	X	E	J	L	O	M	S	S	G	A	A	U	E	D	T	E
J	T	S	D	S	X	E	M	C	H	N	B	I	R	T	R	A	R
Y	S	P	A	G	H	E	T	T	I	B	L	R	E	I	O	X	R
Q	P	I	Z	Z	A	K	U	I	P	U	E	G	O	C	B	I	Y
K	C	U	R	T	A	I	N	A	N	O	R	A	K	S	E	N	E

transport

bus

_____

_____

_____

_____

_____

_____

sport

athletics

_____

_____

_____

_____

_____

_____

_____

_____

_____

room

_____

_____

_____

_____

_____

_____

clothes

_____

_____

_____

_____

_____

_____

food

_____

_____

_____

_____

_____

_____

_____

Unit 4

New words ▶ pp. 68 – 69

Sue liebt Dan, aber Dan will mit Kim **ausgehen**.
Sue loves Dan, but Dan wants to _____ Kim.

ein amerikanischer **Film** aus den 70er-Jahren
an American _____ from the 1970s

Berlin hat 3,5 Millionen **Einwohner**.
The _____ of Berlin is 3.5 million.

ein 25 **Quadratmeter** großes Wohnzimmer
a 25 _____ living room

Es ist so kalt heute – **minus** 8 Grad.
It's so cold today – _____ 8 degrees.

Es war sehr heiß gestern – 35 Grad **plus**.
It was very hot yesterday – 35 degrees _____ .

35 Grad **Celsius**! Das ist wirklich heiß.
35 degrees _____ ! That's really hot.

Du brauchst einen Schlafanzug für die **Schlafparty**.
You need pyjamas for the _____ .

Am Wochenende gehen wir **richtig spät** ins Bett.
We go to bed _____ at weekends.

Aktivitäten **im Freien** machen im Sommer Spaß.
_____ activities are fun in summer.

Jagt eure Katze auch Mäuse?
Does your cat _____ mice too?

Ist **Schneeschuhwandern** dasselbe wie Skifahren?
Is _____ the same as skiing?

Auf diesem Fluss habe ich gelernt, **Kanu** zu **fahren**.
I learned to _____ on this river.

1 Lost words

Ergänze die Sätze mit den Wörtern im Feuerwerk.

1 I was really surprised ____*at*____ the size of the Canadian forests.

2 Moles are wild animals that live _____ the ground.

3 Jack is in hospital for an operation _____ his knee.

4 If you wait _____ Sue arrives, you'll be able to say hello.

5 I love being _____ the clouds when I travel by plane.

6 We live in the city centre, close _____ the big shops.

7 Mike was very upset _____ the bad news.

8 Anna moved her English books _____ a higher shelf.

9 There was no bridge at the river, so I couldn't get _____ .

10 Last night I dreamed _____ a holiday in Canada.

below
at
on
across
to
about
above
about
onto
until

2 School words

Ergänze die fehlenden Wörter. Finde das „geheime Wort" und übersetze es.

1 _b o a r d_   Jack, can you write the answers on the ★ please?

2 _ _ _ _ _   We have lots of good singers in our school ★.

3 _ _ _ _ _ _   I'm in the seventh ★ this year.

4 _ _ _ _ _ _ _ _   How many ★ are there at your school? – About 800.

5 _ _ _ _ _ _ _   In ★ you learn about the past.

6 _ _ _ _ _ _ _   And in ★ you learn about flowers, animals, etc.

7 _ _ _ _ _ _   I need a ★, not a pen.

8 _ _ _ _ _ _ _   We have the same ★ for PE and English: Mr Hill.

9 _ _ _ _   In ★ you learn how to draw and paint.

10 _ _ _ _ _   In English we have to write an ★ about our hobbies.

The secret word is: *Englisch* _____   *Deutsch* _____

3 Word pairs

Welche Wörter passen zusammen?

New words ▸ pp. 70 – 71

Das Radio ist zu laut – **mach** es bitte **leiser**!	The radio's too loud – please _____ it _____ !
Die Musik ist OK, aber ich hasse den **Liedtext**.	The song sounds OK, but I hate the _____ .
ein **lockerer** Typ, der nie wütend wird	an _____ type who never gets angry
Unsere Eltern sind **streng**, aber fair.	Our parents are _____ , but fair.
Gib das Geld vorsichtig aus! **Verschwende** es nicht!	Spend the money carefully! Don't _____ it!
Schicke Jugendliche tragen oft die **neueste** Mode.	Trendy teens often wear the _____ fashion.
Im Flugzeug muss man **Handys** ausschalten.	You must turn off _____ on a plane.
Erwachsene müssen mehr als Kinder zahlen.	_____ have to pay more than children.
Dieser **altmodische** Hut gehörte Opa.	This _____ hat was grandpa's.
Ich mag **moderne** Städte lieber als alte Städte.	I like _____ cities more than old cities.
Lache nicht **über** Kinder, die anders sind.	Don't _____ kids who are different.
Ich wollte nicht viel machen, nur **rumhängen**.	I didn't want to do much, just _____ .
einkaufen im **Einkaufszentrum**	go shopping at the _____
Ich muss **bis spätestens** 8 Uhr zu Hause sein.	I have to be home _____ eight o'clock.
Wir wohnten in einer **Hütte** in den Bergen.	We stayed in a _____ in the mountains.
Am Wochenende stehe ich **erst um** 11 Uhr auf.	At weekends, I do ___ get up _____ 11 o'clock.
Hey **Leute**! Geht nicht ohne mich.	Hey _____ ! Don't go without me.

4 One or two letters?

Trage die fehlenden Buchstaben ein:
d *oder* **dd**, **f** *oder* **ff**, **n** *oder* **nn**

g/gg	re_gg_ae, be____in, lan____uage, bi____est, fo____, fo____y
l/ll	ce____phone, adu____t, unti____, ta____ent, mode____, pu____over
m/mm	co____unity, swi____er, wo____an, gra____ar, mo____ent, thermo____eter
p/pp	po____ulation, sho____ing, pe____er, su____orter, re____resent, disa____ear
r/rr	tomo____ow, ma____ied, guita____, ti____ed, hu____y, di____ections
s/ss	e____cape, e____ay, gla____es, gue____, hu____band, i____land
t/tt	bo____le, wa____er, pre____y, wea____her, spaghe____i

5 Vocabulary network

*Vervollständige das Wörternetz.
Die Verben, die auf den Zetteln
fehlen, bringt der Geier.
Die anderen Wörter findest du
im Sand.*

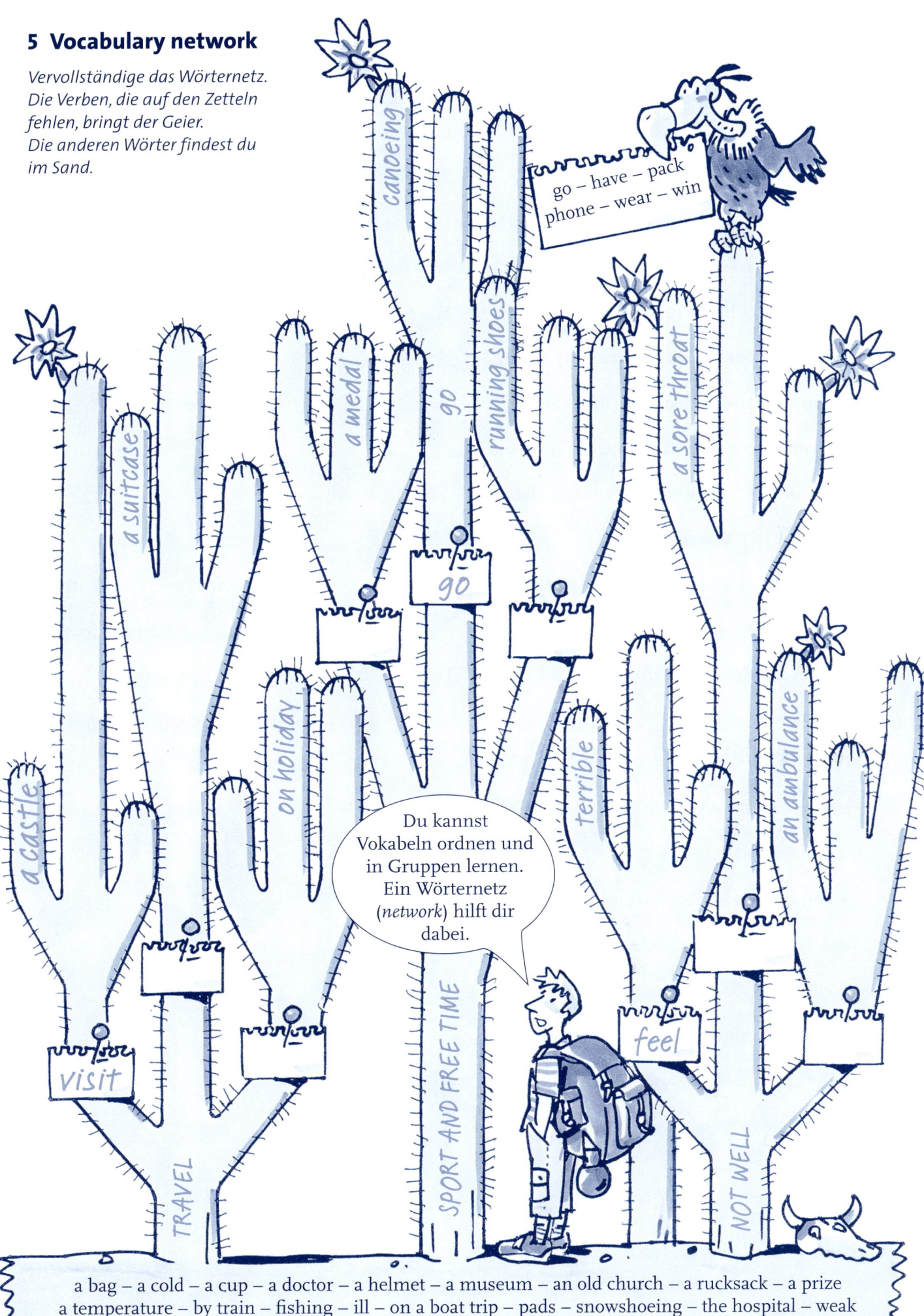

go – have – pack
phone – wear – win

Du kannst
Vokabeln ordnen und
in Gruppen lernen.
Ein Wörternetz
(*network*) hilft dir
dabei.

a bag – a cold – a cup – a doctor – a helmet – a museum – an old church – a rucksack – a prize
a temperature – by train – fishing – ill – on a boat trip – pads – snowshoeing – the hospital – weak

New words ▸ pp. 72 – 73

Ist Ontario die größte **Provinz** Kanadas?	Is Ontario Canada's largest _____ ?
Ist diese Musik **traditionell** oder modern?	Is this music _____ or modern?
Wir müssen uns gegen Diebe **schützen**.	We must _____ ourselves against thieves.
Haben viele Menschen den **Angriff** überlebt?	Did many people survive the _____ ?
Warum **greifen** Bären Menschen an?	Why do bears _____ people?
Der Zug fährt um **genau** 18 Uhr ab.	The train leaves at _____ 6 pm.
Es gibt keine gute **Begründung** für die Jagd.	There's no good _____ for hunting.
Gib mir nicht **die Schuld** für deine Fehler!	Don't _____ me for your mistakes!
gute **Argumente** in einer Diskussion **vorbringen**	_____ good _____ in a discussion
Tim stimmt mir zu, aber Jo **ist anderer Meinung**.	Tim agrees with me, but Jo _____ .
Wer ist der **Leiter** dieser Gruppe?	Who's the _____ of this group?
Ein **Mikrofon** macht deine Stimme lauter.	A _____ makes your voice louder.
Wir kennen **uns** – wir sind alte Freunde.	We know _____ – we're old friends.
Lass uns den **Refrain** zusammen singen.	Let's sing the _____ together.

6 Spot the mistakes

In jedem Satz sind zwei Fehler.
Unterstreiche und korrigiere sie.

1 When <u>childs</u> are young they often has teddy bears.   *children* _____

2 Bears can look realy sweet and lots off people love them.   _____ _____

3 But they are allso large and very danger animals.   _____ _____

4 They usualy hunt at night or in the errly morning.   _____ _____

5 Bears can ran quickly and they are great swimers.   _____ _____

6 It's very interresting to watch how a bear catches salmons.   _____ _____

7 It stand in the river and waits quitely for a long time.   _____ _____

8 When the bare sees a fish it jump and catches it.   _____ _____

7 Word search

Im Rätsel sind 30 Tiere versteckt.
Finde und schreibe sie auf. (↓ →)

rabbit _____ _____

R	A	B	B	I	T	H	Y	C	H	U	I	B	G	B
L	N	R	O	N	P	E	W	H	O	C	C	T	I	U
T	W	F	G	P	N	D	H	I	R	D	R	U	R	D
I	U	R	S	A	M	G	A	C	S	Y	O	R	A	G
G	S	W	A	R	O	E	M	K	E	X	C	K	F	I
E	N	F	L	R	L	H	S	E	L	P	O	E	F	E
R	A	R	M	O	E	O	T	N	E	I	D	Y	E	S
K	K	O	O	T	P	G	E	U	P	G	I	X	F	Q
Q	E	G	N	P	C	I	R	S	H	Q	L	C	O	U
R	K	A	N	G	A	R	O	O	A	I	E	O	X	I
H	B	W	N	Z	F	L	I	O	N	Q	S	W	Y	R
I	E	S	W	A	L	R	U	S	T	A	H	J	U	R
N	A	K	W	O	O	D	P	E	C	K	E	R	S	E
O	R	F	S	M	O	U	S	E	R	A	E	L	U	L
M	O	N	K	E	Y	G	O	W	H	I	P	P	O	W

_____ _____

_____ _____

_____ _____

_____ _____

_____ _____

_____ _____

_____ _____

_____ _____

_____ _____

_____ _____

_____ _____

_____ _____

8 Pronunciation

In jeder Wortgruppe gibt es bei zwei Wörtern stumme Buchstaben. Finde die Wörter und streiche die stummen Buchstaben durch.

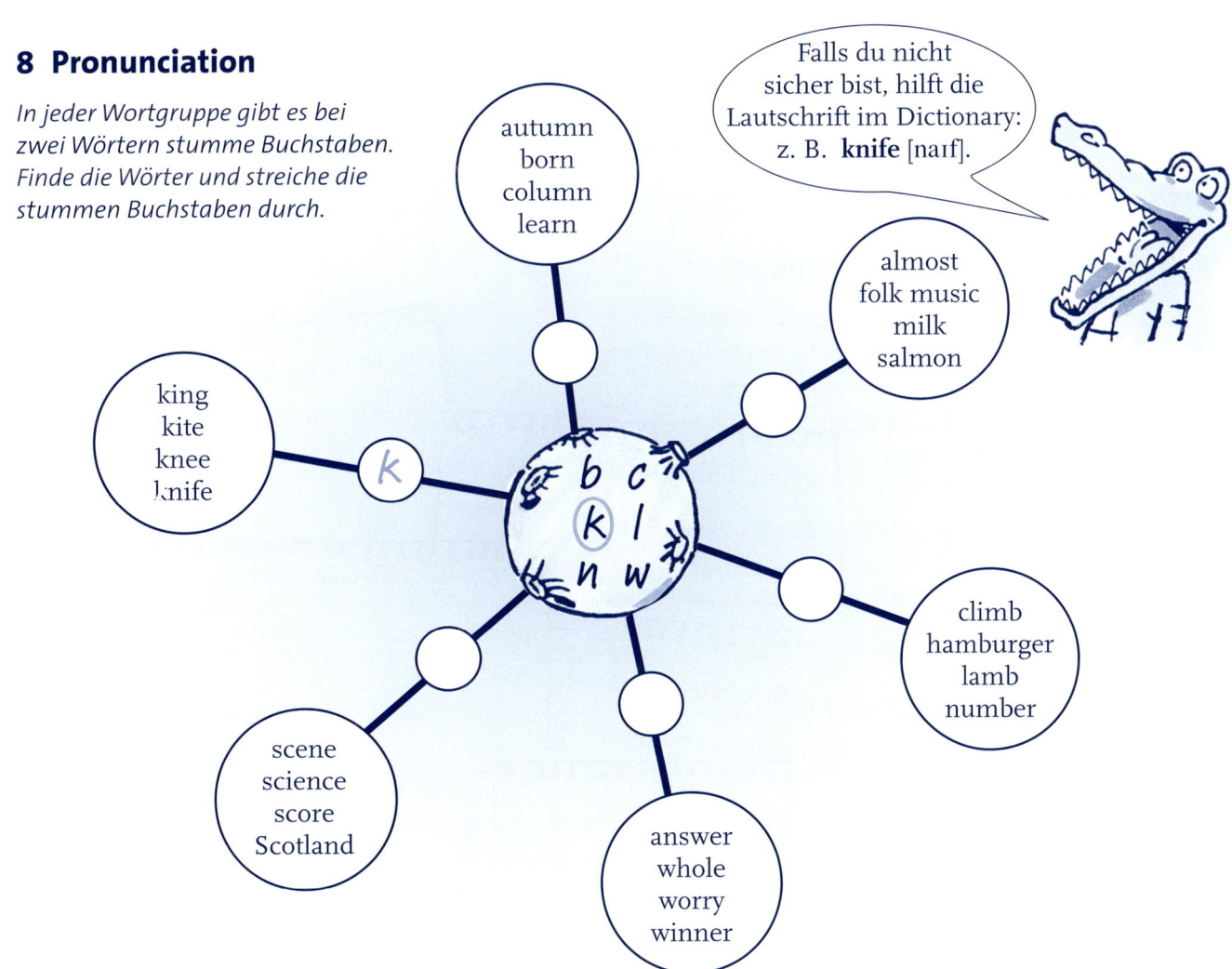

Falls du nicht sicher bist, hilft die Lautschrift im Dictionary: z. B. **knife** [naɪf].

autumn
born
column
learn

almost
folk music
milk
salmon

king
kite
knee
knife

k

b c K l n w

climb
hamburger
lamb
number

scene
science
score
Scotland

answer
whole
worry
winner

New words ▸ pp. 76 – 80

Über 10 **Prozent** der Briten leben in London.	Over 10 _____ of the British live in London.
Die Zimmer kosten 50 Euro **pro** Nacht.	The rooms cost 50 euros _____ night.
ein 30 **Kilogramm** schwerer Hund	a 30 – _____ dog
tolerant gegenüber dem Standpunkt anderer	_____ of other people's point of view
Hotelgäste mögen die **entspannte** Atmosphäre.	Hotel guests like the _____ atmosphere.
Das darfst du nicht – es ist gegen die **Regeln**!	You musn't do that – it's against the _____ !
Es ist **verrückt**, im Winter nur ein T-Shirt zu tragen.	It's _____ to wear just a T-shirt in winter.
Ich muss laufen – die Busfahrer **streiken**.	I have to walk – the bus drivers are on _____ .
Ein **Walross** ist ein großes Tier, das im Meer lebt.	A _____ is a big animal that lives in the sea.
ein Baby in eine **Decke** legen	put a baby in a _____
Brainstormt so viele Ideen wie möglich!	_____ as many ideas as possible!
Stellt bitte keine **dummen** Fragen.	Please don't ask _____ questions.
Vokabeln vor dem Test **wiederholen**	_____ vocabulary before the test
Wolltest du nicht deinen Aufsatz **überarbeiten**?	Didn't you want to _____ your essay?
die **Rechtschreibung** in einem Aufsatz überprüfen	check the _____ in an essay

9 Words with different meanings

Finde in der Liste die passenden Wörter zu den Paaren 1–6.
Trage sie ein und unterstreiche die deutschen Entsprechungen.

3
a) Der Zug fährt um 17.30 ab.
b) Wir trainieren dreimal die Woche.
_____

2
a) ein Bild ausmalen
b) eine schöne Farbe
_____

1
a) auf der Nordseite des Platzes
b) 20 Quadratmeter

square
_____

5
a) Ich gehe einmal pro Woche schwimmen
b) Kinder mussten einst in Fabriken arbeiten
_____

argument
colour
date
final
once
square
train

4
a) Was für ein Datum haben wir heute?
b) Kim hat eine Verabredung mit Alex.
_____

a) das Endspiel
b) die letzte Minute
_____

6

7
a) ein böser Streit
b) eine gute Begründung
_____

10 Odd word out

Finde und unterstreiche das Wort, das nicht passt.

1 kilometre – minute – metre – centimetre

2 lyrics – drawing – photo – picture

3 seven – minus – eight – nine

4 cellphone – text message – mobile – telephone

5 eyes – build – glasses – see

6 adults – children – teenagers – sledges

7 mall – gig – supermarket – department store

8 journey – ride – trip – bottle

11 The fourth word

Welches Wort fehlt hier?

1 centimetre – metre / metre – _____

2 murder – murderer / lead – _____

3 he – they / himself – _____

4 green – colour / two – _____

5 parrot – bird /piano – _____

6 days – month / months – _____

7 day – sun / night – _____

8 man – men / knife – _____

12 More about ... traditional Inuit hunting

Vervollständige den Text mit Wörtern aus der Box.

The Inuit live in Greenland and in the north of Canada, where winter *temperatures* (1) can be minus 40 degrees Celsius. So it's _____ (2) too cold to have farm animals or to grow food. That's why hunting and _____ (3) were once a very big part of Inuit life. The meat of sea animals like the walrus or the whale, or of _____ (4) animals like the polar bear, was traditional Inuit food. And of course, hunting wasn't _____ (5) important for food. The Inuit could also use animal *skins to make clothes. In the past, when the Inuit hunted sea animals they used a *kayak*, a _____ (6) of canoe. And on land they _____ (7) sledges with dogs. A team of dogs could easily pull 20 kilos. And dogs _____ (8) smell very well too, so they could help the Inuit to find the animals. Sometimes a hunting trip took a few days, so the Inuit often _____ (9) little igloos when they needed a place to sleep at night. Inside an igloo, the temperature could be _____ (10) 20 degrees Celsius when it was only minus 40 outside.

skin = Fell

> built could fishing used
> land much kind plus
> just temperatures

New words ▶ pp. 81–82

Es ist billiger zu **zelten**, als im Hotel zu wohnen.	It's cheaper to _____ than to stay at a hotel.
Hat jemand angerufen, **während** ich weg war?	Did anybody call _____ I was out?
Es gab ein Feuer, aber wir konnten **entkommen**.	There was a fire, but we were able to _____ .
Wir müssen sie vor den Gefahren **warnen**.	We have to _____ them about the dangers.
Wo kann ich lernen, mit einem Kanu zu **paddeln**?	Where can I learn to _____ a canoe?
Diese **Stromschnellen** sind für Boote gefährlich.	These _____ are dangerous for boats.

13 Number crossword

Gleiche Zahlen sind gleiche Buchstaben. Die angegebenen Lösungen helfen dir, das gesamte Rätsel zu lösen. Alle Wörter sind in dieser Unit neu.

Wo im Rätsel findet man das englische Wort für ...

Provinz	_m across_	Erwachsene(r)	_____
Hütte	_h down_	schützen	_____
Jagd	_____	streng	_____
Angriff	_____	Einwohnerzahl	_____

14 Word groups

*Trage die Wörter aus der Wolke
in die richtigen Sterne ein.*

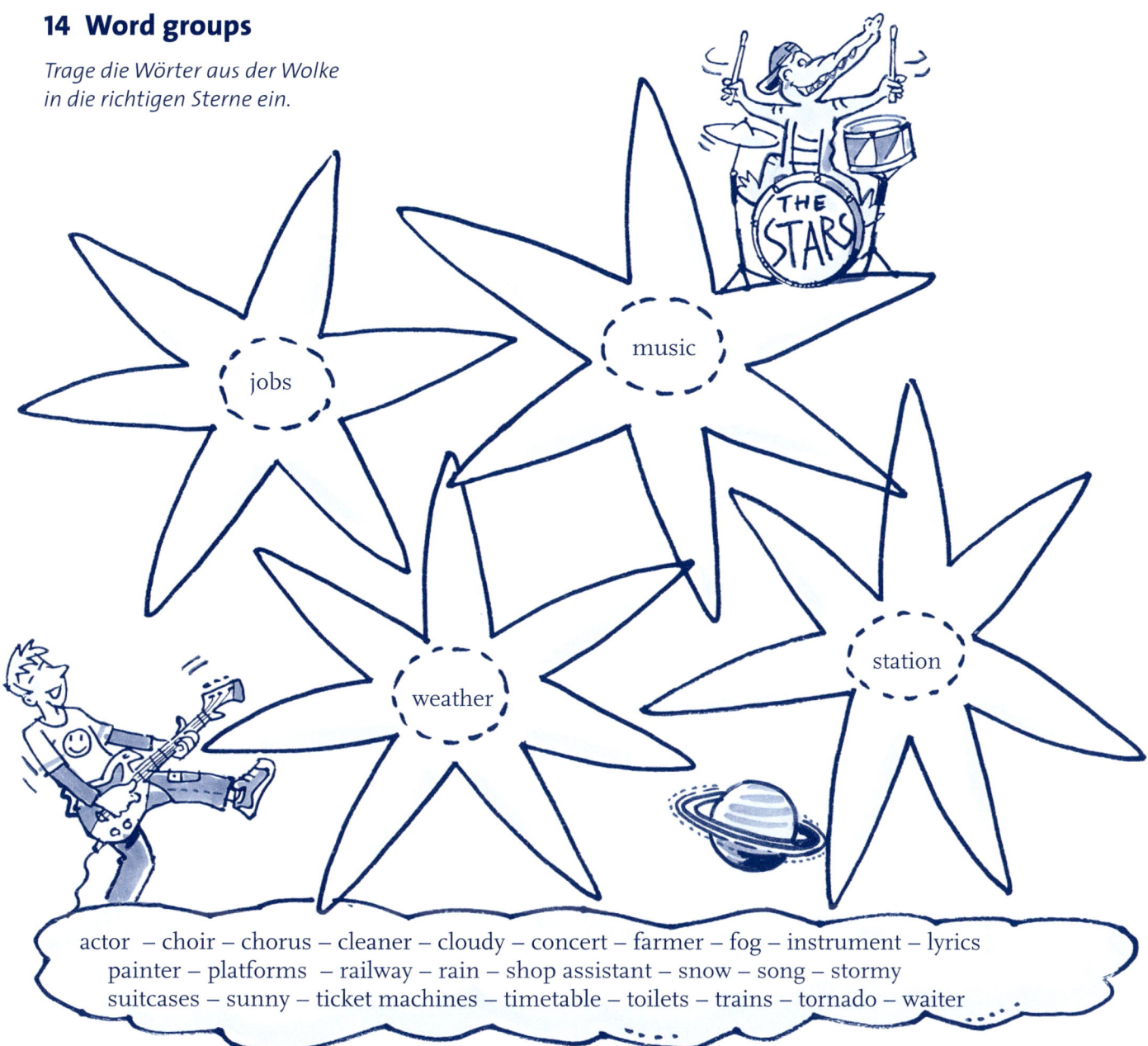

jobs

music

weather

station

actor – choir – chorus – cleaner – cloudy – concert – farmer – fog – instrument – lyrics
painter – platforms – railway – rain – shop assistant – snow – song – stormy
suitcases – sunny – ticket machines – timetable – toilets – trains – tornado – waiter

15 Opposites

Trage die Gegenteile der fettgedruckten Wörter in die Lücken ein.

1 have **tolerant** / _____ parents

2 Do you really **agree** / _____ with me?

3 wears **old-fashioned** / _____ clothes

4 turn the music **down** / _____

5 **plus** / _____ 10 degrees Celsius

6 **enter** / _____ the classroom

7 at the **top** / _____ of the shelf

8 **forget** / _____ an important date

9 There are 90 **arrivals** / _____ every day.

10 find a **husband** / _____

11 an **exciting** / a _____ film

12 a really **hot** / _____ day

13 a **clean** / _____ city

14 Wait **downstairs** / _____ in your room!

Unit 5

New words ▸ pp. 88–89

Wann werden sie die Gewinner **bekanntgeben**?
When will they _____ the winners?

Das musst du selbst entscheiden.
_____

Diese Zeitung hat einen tollen Sport**teil**.
This paper has a great sport _____ .

Ein **Redakteur** überprüft und korrigiert Texte.
An _____ checks and corrects texts.

Was **produziert** diese Fabrik?
What does this factory _____ ?

Willst du den Artikel **veröffentlichen**?
Do you want to _____ the article?

Was wäre besser: ein Foto oder eine **Zeichnung**?
What would be better: photo or a _____ ?

Setze dich mit ihm über das Telefon in Verbindung.
_____ him by phone.

Papa sitzt jeden Tag am Schreibtisch im **Büro**.
Dad sits at his desk in the _____ every day.

Unser Wohltätigkeitsbasar war wieder ein **Erfolg**.
Our jumble sale was a _____ again.

Erfolgreiche Schriftsteller verkaufen viele Bücher.
_____ writers sell lots of books.

Ich trage **Kopfhörer**, wenn ich Musik spiele.
I wear _____ when I play music.

Wie groß ist dein Computer**bildschirm**?
How big is your computer _____ ?

Was **hältst du von** deinen neuen Nachbarn?
What do you _____ about your new neighbours?

1 Pronunciation

Ordne die Wörter aus der Box der richtigen Aussprachegruppe zu.

ʊ   juː   ʌ

~~bully~~ comp~~u~~ter comm~~u~~nity exc~~u~~se f~~u~~ll ~~fun~~ g~~u~~n h~~u~~ge men~~u~~
p~~u~~blish p~~u~~ll p~~u~~t p~~u~~sh s~~u~~gar s~~u~~mmer t~~u~~nnel t~~u~~be tr~~u~~mpet

bully _____   computer _____   fun _____

_____   _____   _____

_____   _____   _____

_____   _____   _____

_____   _____   _____

2 Last letter – first letter

*Der letzte Buchstabe von jedem Wort ist
gleichzeitig der erste des nächsten Wortes.*

1 Refrain
2 Erfolg
3 erfolgreich
4 Leiter, Führer
5 Stromschnellen
6 Rechtschreibung
7 Oma
8 ankündigen
9 Redakteur
10 überarbeiten, wiederholen
11 elektrisch
12 verrückt
13 ja
14 Abschnitt

3 The fourth word

Welches Wort wird hier gesucht?

1 banana – fruit / pea – _____

2 lunch – meal / chicken curry – _____

3 salmon – fish / woodpecker – _____

4 castle – building / armchair – _____

5 dishwasher – machine / piano – _____

6 Britain – island / Uranus – _____

7 seven – number / pink – _____

8 song – music / painting – _____

4 Making phrases

Vervollständige die Audrücke mit einem Verb aus der Box.

1 *settle* down in a new city

2 _____ down the radio a bit

3 _____ people about the bears in the forest

4 _____ what you read in the newspaper

5 _____ with my partner's ideas

6 _____ up in a big city

7 _____ up a word I don't know

8 _____ from a fire in a hotel

grow disagree turn believe settle escape look warn

New words ▸ p. 90

Überfliegt den Text, aber lest ihn nicht im Detail. _____ the text, but don't read it in detail.

Gute Broschüren haben **nützliche** Informationen. Good brochures have _____ information.

Die **Haupt**einkaufsstraße ist sehr belebt. The _____ shopping street is very busy.

Die neuen Wörter sind in **Fettdruck**. The new words are in _____ .

Ist das eine gute **Bildunterschrift** für dieses Foto? Is that a good _____ for this photo?

Wann bist du heute Morgen **aufgewacht**? When did you _____ this morning?

Bitte **weck** mich morgen um sieben Uhr. Please _____ me tomorrow at 7 o'clock.

Dieser **Radiosender** spielt immer tolle Musik. This _____ always plays great music.

Ich brauche **Stille, damit** ich lesen kann. I need _____ I can read.

5 Word building

Verbinde ein Wort aus den Steinen mit einem Wort aus der Liste. Trage die deutsche Übersetzung ein.

> Wenn man Nomen miteinander verbindet, schreibt man sie mal auseinander, mal zusammen.

> Eine Regel gibt es leider nicht. Also merkt euch die Einzelfälle!

Stones: bold · text · class · running · great · snow · semi · chat · black · wheel

1 _bold_ print _Fettdruck_

2 _____ bear _____

3 _____ room _____

4 _____ shoes _____

5 _____ message _____

6 _semi-_ final _____

7 _____ grandfather _____

8 _class_ room _____

9 _____ shoes _____

10 _____ chair _____

6 Word families

Finde die passenden Verben zu den angegebenen Nomen.

1 announcement – _announce_

2 revision – _____

3 spelling – _____

4 drawing – _____

5 ending – _____

6 life – _____

7 attack – _____

8 supporter – _____

9 hunter – _____

10 rapper – _____

7 Hour glasses

Übersetze die Wörter und trage sie in die passende Sanduhr ein.

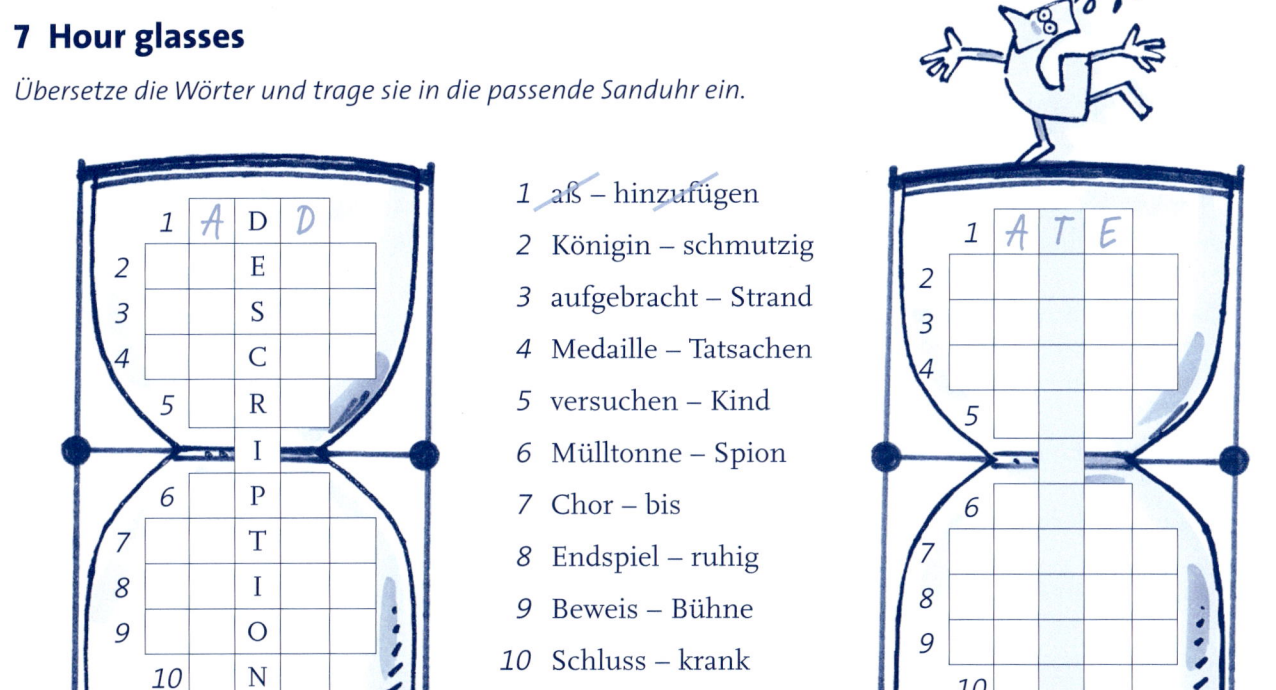

1	A	D	D
2		E	
3		S	
4		C	
5		R	
		I	
6		P	
7		T	
8		I	
9		O	
10		N	

1 aß – hinzufügen

2 Königin – schmutzig

3 aufgebracht – Strand

4 Medaille – Tatsachen

5 versuchen – Kind

6 Mülltonne – Spion

7 Chor – bis

8 Endspiel – ruhig

9 Beweis – Bühne

10 Schluss – krank

1	A	T	E
2			
3			
4			
5			
6			
7			
8			
9			
10			

Das geheime Wort in der rechten Sanduhr heißt: Englisch _____

Deutsch _____

8 Word ladder

Gehe von unten nach oben, indem du bei jeder Sprosse einen Buchstaben veränderst.

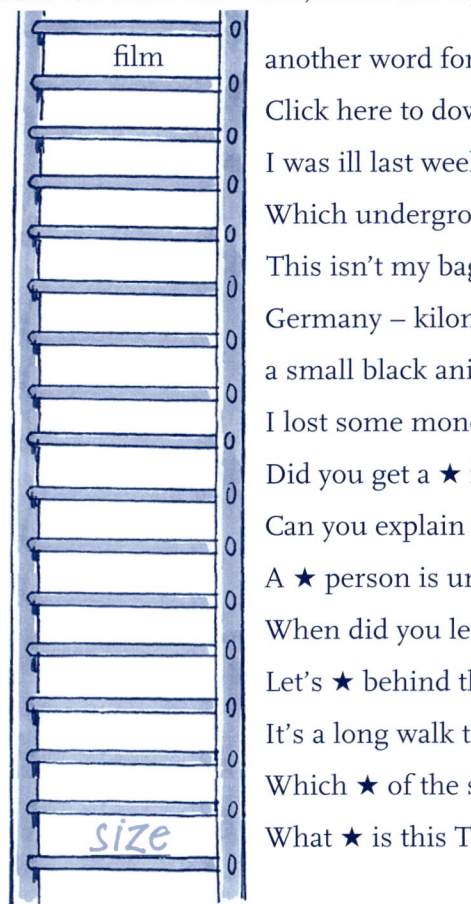

film

another word for movie

Click here to download the sound ★.

I was ill last week but I'm ★ again now.

Which underground ★ goes to St Paul's Cathedral?

This isn't my bag – ★ is blue, not black

Germany – kilometre, Britain and America – ★

a small black animal that lives under the ground

I lost some money because there was a ★ in my pocket.

Did you get a ★ in the school play?

Can you explain this grammar ★ please?

A ★ person is unfriendly to other people.

When did you learn to ★ a horse?

Let's ★ behind this wall. Then nobody will see us.

It's a long walk to the water when the ★ is out.

Which ★ of the street is number 47?

What ★ is this T-shirt? Medium or large?

size

New words ▸ p. 91

Wir fanden keine Antwort auf das **Rätsel**.	We didn't find an answer to the _____ .
Er trägt eine schwarze **Leder**jacke.	He's wearing a black _____ jacket.
Kirchenorgeln haben sehr viele **Pfeifen**.	Church organs have got lots of _____ .
Eine Flasche **ragte aus** der Einkaufstasche **heraus**.	A bottle _____ of the shopping bag.
Fleisch muss man im Kühlschrank **aufbewahren**.	You have to _____ meat in the fridge.
Er **drückte** ihre Hand und lächelte.	He _____ her hand and smiled.
Hast du dich in der neuen Wohnung **eingewöhnt**?	Have you _____ in the new flat.
Bist du auch **gut in** Französisch?	Are you _____ French too?
Warum habt ihr euch **entschieden**, umzuziehen?	Why did you _____ to move?
Er verließ die Schule im **Alter** von 16.	He left school at the _____ of 16.
Es tut mir leid, aber die Karten sind **ausverkauft**.	I'm sorry, but the tickets are _____ .

9 Definitions

*Vervollständige die Definitionen mit Wörtern
aus den Mauersteinen. Trage die richtigen Wörter
aus Kens Zeitung in die rechte Spalte ein.*

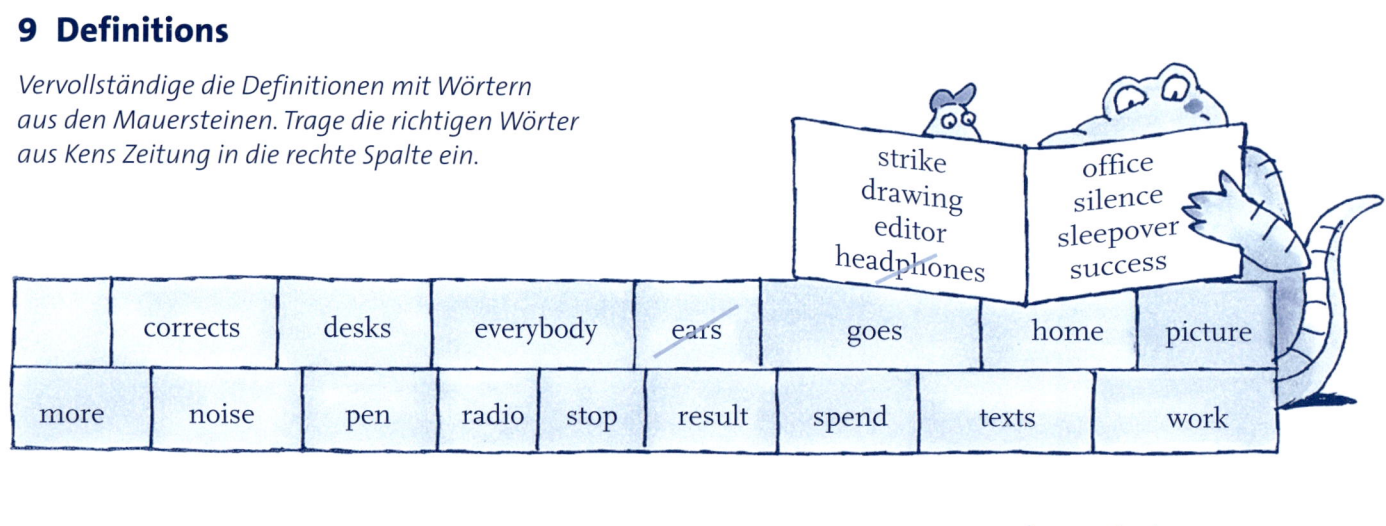

strike drawing editor headphones office silence sleepover success

corrects	desks	everybody	~~ears~~	goes	home	picture

more	noise	pen	radio	stop	result	spend	texts	work

1 Wear these over your *ears* to listen to an mp3 player or the _____ .   *headphones*

2 when people _____ work because they want _____ money   _____

3 when you _____ the night at a friend's _____   _____

4 someone who checks and _____ articles and other _____   _____

5 a room with _____ and computers where people sit and _____   _____

6 a _____ that you make with a pencil or _____   _____

7 when something _____ well and there's a good _____   _____

8 when _____ is quiet and there is no _____   _____

10 Words in pictures: fruit and vegetables

a) *Wie heißt das abgebildete Obst und Gemüse?*
   Trage die Wörter in die nummerierten Lücken ein.

1 <u>bright</u> long <u>red</u>	*tomatoes*	6 delicious German neat _____
2 delicious windy forest _____		7 bright round orange _____
3 sweet Spanish spicy _____		8 healthy green empty _____
4 short hard green _____		9 delicious sunny new _____
5 big grey garden _____		10 long yellow German _____

b) *2 von 3 Adjektiven passen zu den Wörtern, die du eingetragen hast. Unterstreiche sie.*

11 Opposites

Trage die Gegenteile der fett gedruckten Wörter in die Lücken ein.

1 the **best** / _____ book I've ever read

2 be **good** / _____ at French

3 at the **bottom** / _____ of the street

4 **bright** / _____ colours

5 a **healthy** / an _____ meal

6 **modern** / _____ furniture

7 arrive **early** / _____ for the lesson

8 a **tidy** / an _____ room

9 **in front of** / _____ the house

10 a good **question** / _____

11 live **above** / _____ ground

12 ask about **departure** / _____ times

13 look **left** / _____

14 **remember** / _____ to phone a friend

New words ▸ *pp. 92–93*

Wie lang sind die Sommer**ferien** in Kanada?	How long is summer _____ in Canada?
ein Projekt **auf den Weg bringen**	_____ a project _____
Ich glaube, Alex ist in Chris **verknallt**.	I think Alex _____ Chris.
400 Meilen! Ist die Fahrt wirklich **so** lang?	400 miles! Is the journey really _____ long?
Der März ist der Monat, den ich **am wenigsten** mag!	March is the month I like _____!
Hab ich dir schon unser Foto**album** gezeigt?	Have I showed you our photo _____ yet?
In Schottland hört man oft den **Dudelsack**.	You often hear the _____ in Scotland.
Was ist deine Traum**karriere**?	What's you dream _____?
Ich möchte ein **Musiker** in einer Band werden.	I'd like to be a _____ in a band.
Wir können in ein Konzert oder in die **Oper** gehen.	We can go to a concert or to the _____.
Ich habe viele CDs, aber keine **Schallplatten**.	I have lots of CDs, but no _____.
Willst du das Konzert live **aufnehmen**?	Do you want to _____ the concert live?
Wird die Band eine neue CD **herausbringen**?	Is the band going to _____ a new CD?
Hast du ihre neue **Single** schon gehört?	Have you heard their new _____ yet?
Wie viele **Titel** gibts auf der CD?	How many _____ are there on the CD?
Passt die **Melodie** wirklich zum Songtext?	Does the _____ really go with the lyrics?
ein **Musikinstrument** spielen lernen	learn to play a _____

12 The best word

Finde das Wort in der Strickleiter, das am besten in die Lücke passt.

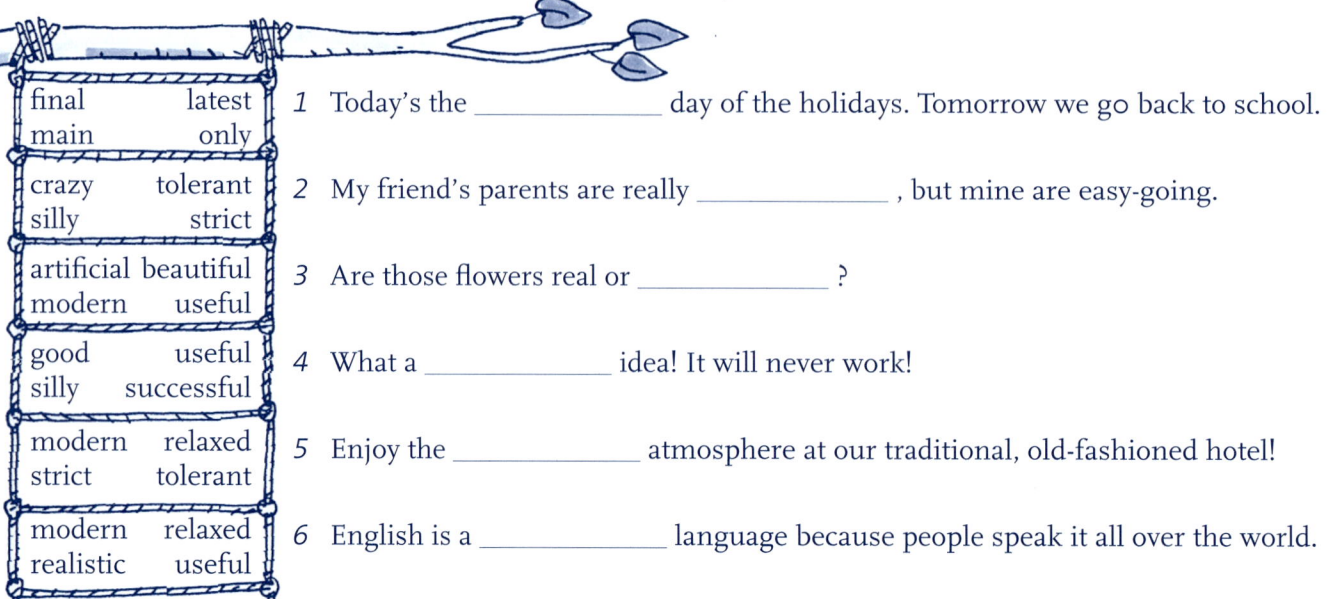

final latest main only	1 Today's the _____ day of the holidays. Tomorrow we go back to school.
crazy tolerant silly strict	2 My friend's parents are really _____ , but mine are easy-going.
artificial beautiful modern useful	3 Are those flowers real or _____ ?
good useful silly successful	4 What a _____ idea! It will never work!
modern relaxed strict tolerant	5 Enjoy the _____ atmosphere at our traditional, old-fashioned hotel!
modern relaxed realistic useful	6 English is a _____ language because people speak it all over the world.

13 Hidden words

Ergänze die Wortgruppen, indem du Wörter mit Buchstaben der Wörter „*musical instruments*" bildest.

14 Word search - The media

15 englische Begriffe aus dem Wortfeld „Medien"
sind im Rätsel versteckt.
Finde sie und übersetze sie ins Deutsche. (↓ →)

newspaper – Zeitung

S	N	E	W	S	P	A	P	E	R	C	I
T	H	R	H	O	L	G	D	H	M	K	T
A	Y	E	E	C	H	A	N	N	E	L	E
T	C	P	A	R	E	C	O	R	D	M	L
I	E	O	D	M	A	G	A	Z	I	N	E
O	L	R	P	E	D	I	T	O	R	M	V
N	L	T	H	C	G	S	Q	G	U	E	I
N	P	R	O	G	R	A	M	M	E	H	S
B	H	N	N	A	R	T	I	C	L	E	I
C	O	X	E	L	B	N	E	W	S	O	O
M	N	G	S	P	U	B	L	I	S	H	N
E	E	X	Q	G	M	O	N	I	T	O	R

New words ▸ pp. 95–96

Es muss funktionieren. Es kann nicht **schiefgehen**.	It must work. It can't _____ .
War es letzte Woche oder **in der Woche zuvor**?	Was it last week or _____ ?
Die **Biografie** erzählt viel über sein Leben.	The _____ tells us a lot about his life.
Wie viele Menschen arbeiten für diese **Firma**?	How many people work for this _____ ?
Kann ich ein **Exemplar** des Berichts haben?	Can I have a _____ of the report?
Fangen Nomen mit **Großbuchstaben** an?	Do nouns start with _____ ?
Ist simple past hier die richtige **Zeit** ?	Is simple past the right _____ here?

15 Word friends

Welche Wörter auf den Steinen passen in die Lücken?

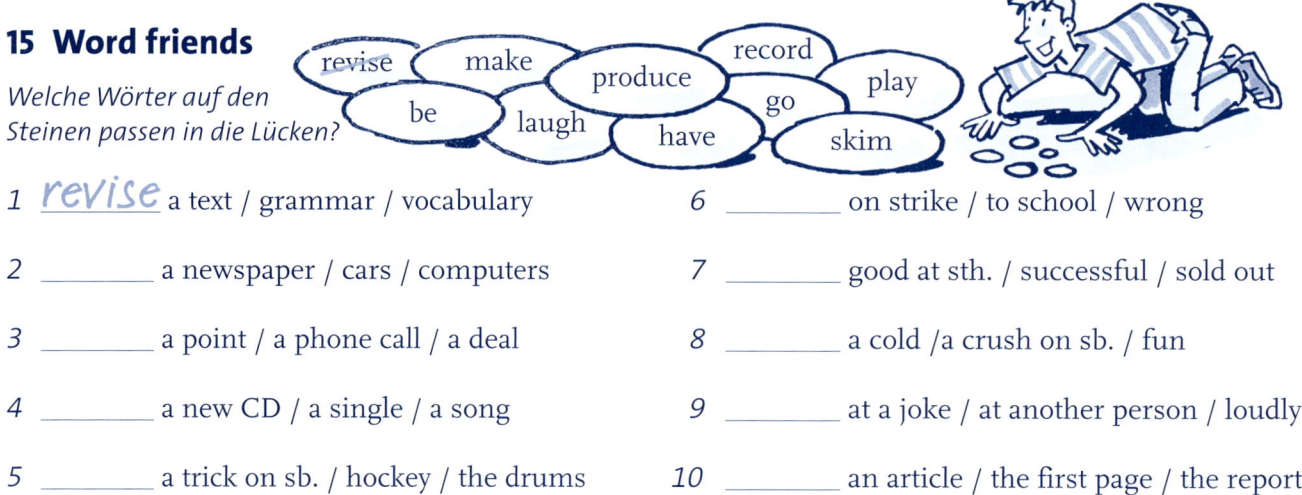

revise · make · produce · record · play · be · laugh · have · go · skim

1 _revise_ a text / grammar / vocabulary

2 _____ a newspaper / cars / computers

3 _____ a point / a phone call / a deal

4 _____ a new CD / a single / a song

5 _____ a trick on sb. / hockey / the drums

6 _____ on strike / to school / wrong

7 _____ good at sth. / successful / sold out

8 _____ a cold / a crush on sb. / fun

9 _____ at a joke / at another person / loudly

10 _____ an article / the first page / the report

16 Scrambled words: American and British English

Die Buchstabenrätsel ergeben Wörter aus dem amerikanischen Englisch. Trage diese und ihre britischen Entsprechungen ein. Die Tipps helfen dir.

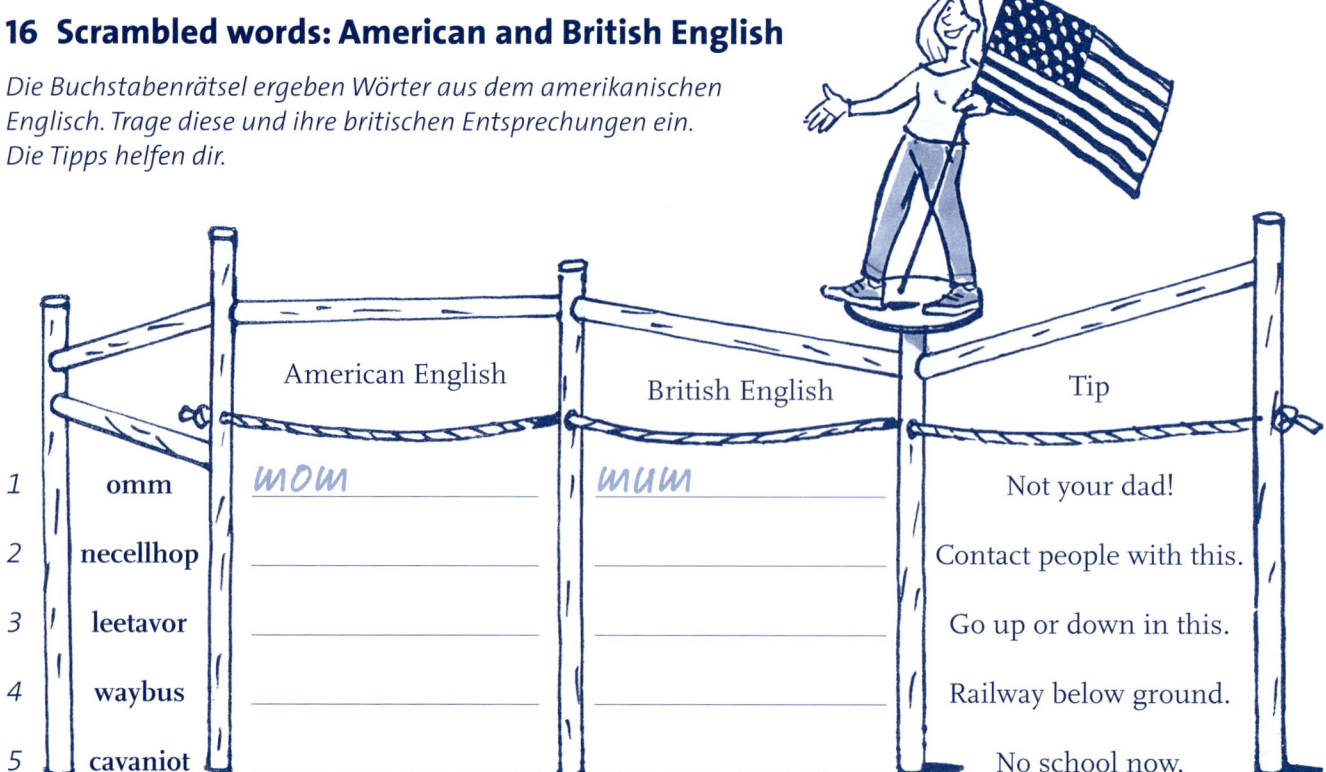

		American English	British English	Tip
1	omm	mom	mum	Not your dad!
2	necellhop	_____	_____	Contact people with this.
3	leetavor	_____	_____	Go up or down in this.
4	waybus	_____	_____	Railway below ground.
5	cavaniot	_____	_____	No school now.

17 Crossword

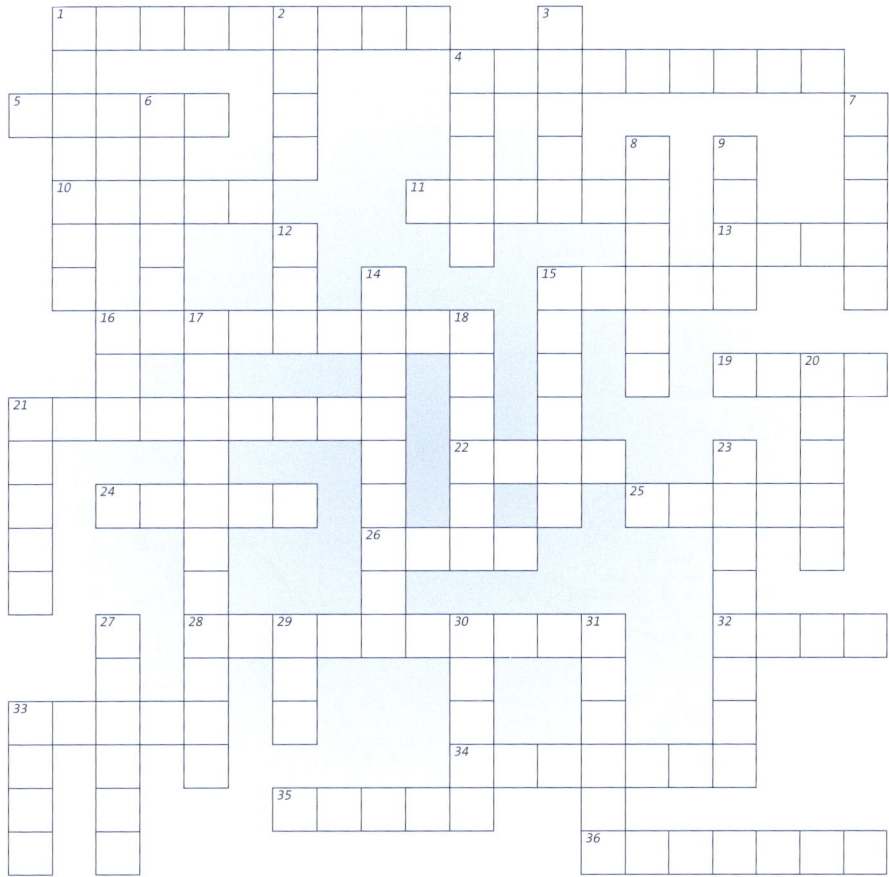

Across →

1 American English for 'mobile phone' (9)
4 the story of a somebody's life (9)
5 You need it to cut bread. (5)
10 The name of the planet we live on. (5)
11 opposite of 'old-fashioned' (6)
13 a name for the underground in London (4)
15 Somebody stole my bike ★ I was in the shop. (5)
16 In this sport, you run, jump, etc. (9)
19 a big shopping centre (4)
21 cupboards, chairs, sofas, wardrobes, etc. (9)
22 60 minutes – an hour /30 minutes – ★ an hour (4)
24 newspapers, magazines, radio, TV, the Internet, etc. (5)
25 a person who trains a sports team (5)
26 the person at work who tells you what you have to do (4)
28 friend – friendly / success – ★ (10)
32 from all ★ England = from every part of England (4)
33 one – once / two – ★ (5)
34 the main city in a country (7)
35 not very clever; stupid (5)
36 a building where you can watch a football match (7)

Down ↓

1 when people play music for an audience (7)
2 very, very big (4)
3 another word for 'film' (5)
4 opposite of 'above' (5)
6 opposite of 'remember' (6)
7 The wife of a king is a ★ . (5)
8 opposite of 'beginning' (6)
9 another word for 'friend' (4)
12 I'm 14. What ★ are you? (3)
14 This gives you information about when buses, trains, etc. arrive and leave. (9)
15 They're round. A car has got four of them. (6)
16 We need it to live. (3)
17 a person who washes and cuts hair (11)
18 the things that tourists like to see (6)
20 Can you turn on the ★ ? It's so dark here. (5)
21 the game to find the winner, always the last game in a series (5)
23 October 3rd is a ★ holiday in Germany (8)
27 a person who checks and corrects texts (6)
29 A team that wins a final often gets this prize. (3)
30 opposite of 'mild' (5)
31 the words of a song (6)
33 make – made / take – ★ (4)

Lösungen

Introduction

1 Crossword

Across: *2* singer, *4* fantastic, *6* favourite,
8 programme, *10* play, *11* show, *12* ticket
Down: *1* song, *2* star, *3* guitar, *4* famous,
5 rehearse, *7* organ, *8* piano, *9* music

2 Verb forms

2 show – showed – shown
3 spend – spent – spent
4 hide – hid – hidden
5 do – did – done
6 take – took – taken
7 fly – flew – flown
8 read – read – read
9 throw – threw – thrown
10 speak – spoke – spoken
11 write – wrote – written
12 ride – rode – ridden

3 Lost words

1 In, *2* of, *3* from, *4* to, *5* at, *6* by, *7* before,
8 between, *9* on, *10* for, *11* over

4 Last letter – first letter

1 drum *2* mixture *3* electric *4* concert
5 trumpet *6* trombone *7* enough *8* half
9 fiddle *10* elevator *11* recorder

5 Word search

piano – Klavier, **organ** – Orgel,
drum – Trommel, **flute** – Querflöte,
recorder – Blockflöte, **fiddle** – Geige,
trombone – Posaune, **trumpet** – Trompete,
guitar – Gitarre, **saxophone** – Saxophon

6 Word groups

places in town
department store, hospital, hostel, leisure
centre, police station, restaurant
jobs
engineer, fireman, paramedic,
photographer, policewoman, waiter
clothes
jacket, pyjamas, sandals, skirt, trousers
animals
deer, frog, hedgehog, mole, squirrel,
woodpecker

Unit 1

1 Definitions

1 four – **wheels**
2 important – country – **capital**
3 places – photos – **sights**
4 woman – king – **queen**
5 spend – hotel – **hostel**
6 live – stage – **concert**

2 Crossword

3 One or two letters?

fiddle, middle, student, hidden, ready, model
afraid, giraffe, traffic, often, difficult, left
anorak, beginning, dinner, tunnel, enemy,
pencil

4 Word ladder

have, **hate**, **gate**, **late**, **lane**, **line**, **fine**, **mine**, **mile**, milk

5 More about ... London Underground

2 because, *3* only, *4* before, *5* and, *6* but, *7* too, *8* when, *9* more, *10* Although

6 Word friends

do: a good job, a project, nothing
dream: about the teacher, every night, on
get: angry, dressed, ready
have: a baby, a cold, enough time
look: after the baby, different, for the money

7 Word search

```
S T R A S S E N B A H N
U D B A H N H O F M U M
E I N S T E I G E N M Q
F L U G H A F E N C S A
L F A H R R A D H I T U
U Q F L U G Z E U G E T
G Q T A X I J Q H F I O
S F A H R P L A N A G P
T Z A U S S T E I G E N
E Z T B U S W U E U N E
I U F M S F A E H R E K
G G B A H N S T E I G T
```

Straßenbahn – tram, **Bahnhof** – station,
einsteigen – get on, **Flughafen** – airport,
Fahrrad – bike, **Flugzeug** – plane, **Taxi** – taxi,
Fahrplan – timetable, **aussteigen** – get off,
Bus – bus, **Fähre** – ferry,
Bahnsteig – platform, **Flugsteig** – gate,
Zug – train, **umsteigen** – change,
Auto – car

8 Word building

1 **dancing lessons** – Tanzstunden
2 **family tree** – Stammbaum,
3 **sports gear** – Sportausrüstung,
4 **sound file** – Tondatei,
5 **ice hockey** – Eishockey,
6 **film star** – Filmstar,
7 **doorbell** – Türklingel,
8 **classroom** – Klassenraum,
9 **homework** – Hausaufgabe,
10 **wheelchair** – Rollstuhl,
11 **firewoman** – Feuerwehrfrau,
12 **weekend** – Wochenende

9 Odd word out

1 museum, *2* dinosaur, *3* CD-player,
4 trendy, *5* meal, *6* ball

10 The best word

1 angry, *2* shy, *3* proud, *4* puzzled,
5 scared, *6* nervous

11 Hidden words

1 meal, *2* air, *3* plane, *4* parent, *5* ear,
6 tram, *7* arm, *8* planet, *9* mail, *10* late,
11 learn

12 Word families

1 dream, *2* explain, *3* install, *4* win, *5* smile,
6 fly, *7* act, *8* laugh, *9* build, *10* describe,
11 rehearse, *12* glue, *13* move, *14* present

13 Pronunciation

e – already, bread, breakfast, dead, head, meant
iː – clean, beach, cheap, eastbound, leave, tea
ɪə – dear, beard, clear, disappear, ear, idea

14 Opposites

1 national, *2* spicy, *3* clean, *4* right,
5 ending, *6* impossible, *7* leave, *8* rich,
9 closed, *10* single

15 Hour glasses

1	F	E	W	
2 W	E	L	S	H
3 C	L	E	A	N
4 F	A	C	T	S
5	A	T	E	
		R		
6	B	I	N	
7 B	A	C	O	N
8 S	K	I	R	T
9 A	F	T	E	R
10	E	Y	E	

1	F	U	N	
2 M	O	N	E	Y
3 T	O	D	A	Y
4 E	N	E	M	Y
5	A	R	M	
		G		
6	A	R	T	
7 S	M	O	K	E
8 F	L	U	T	E
9 S	U	N	N	Y
10	A	D	D	

Das geheime Wort lautet:
Englisch – underground
Deutsch – U-Bahn

16 Picture puzzle

a firework, a dice, a pencil sharpener, a pencil,
a helmet, a sandwich, an apple, a fish

Unit 2

1 Word friends

1 eat, *2* wait, *3* dream, *4* read, *5* speak,
6 listen, *7* know, *8* do, *9* become, *10* keep

2 Words with different meanings

1 **single** – ledig/einfache,
2 **change** – Wechselgeld/umsteigen,
3 **menu** – Speisekarte/Menü,
4 **opposite** – Gegenteil/gegenüber,
5 **work** – arbeiten/funktionieren,
6 **grow** – wachsen/anbauen,
7 **walk** – zu Fuß gehen/Spaziergang

3 Number crossword

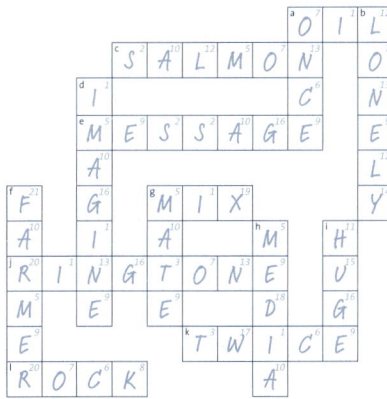

mischen – **g** across
riesig – **i** down
zweimal – **k** across
einsam – **b** down
Medien – **h** down
Kumpel – **g** down
sich (etwas) vorstellen – **d** down
Nachricht – **e** across

4 Scrambled words: school

1 **timetable** – Stundenplan
2 **teacher** – Lehrer,
3 **classmate** – Klassenkamerad/in,
4 **holidays** – (Schul-)Ferien,
5 **board** – Tafel,
6 **science** – Naturwissenschaft,
7 **classroom** – Klassenraum
Das geheime Wort lautet: lessons

5 Last letter – first letter

1 timetable, 2 excited, 3 departure, 4 elephant,
5 take, 6 elevator, 7 rock, 8 key, 9 you,
10 until, 11 lonely, 12 yawn

6 Word groups

farm animals:
chicken, sheep, pig, lamb, horse, cow, turkey
media:
mobile, television, radio, text message, sound
file, magazine, newspaper
public transport:
arrival, departure, timetable, Tube, bus stop,
Travelcard, station

7 Making phrases

1 take, 2 send, 3 check, 4 feed, 5 get off,
6 phone, 7 wait, 8 download

8 Spot the mistakes

1 biger: bigger, ilands: islands,
2 Live: Life, lonly: lonely,
3 have: has, mobil: mobile,
4 write: writes. weak: week,
5 musik: music, webseite: website,
6 taked: took, fotos: photos

9 What are the words

1 allowed, 2 able, 3 able,
4 allowed, 5 able, 6 allowed

10 Word pairs

do – course, **eat** – meal, **pack** – suitcase,
play – trombone, **read** – menu, **send** – message,
turn off – light, **wear** – helmet

11 Lost words

1 unsafe, 2 healthy, 3 untidy,
4 unhealthy, 5 happy, 6 unfriendly

12 Word search: town and country words

H	H	A	R	B	O	U	R	V	P	B	S
I	T	O	W	E	R	F	S	F	A	R	M
L	D	S	Q	U	A	R	E	K	F	N	C
L	Y	E	Z	C	E	Z	A	R	W	P	R
B	M	L	A	A	B	I	S	L	A	N	D
E	O	A	W	N	R	O	A	D	T	Y	G
A	U	K	J	A	I	T	N	Y	G	I	H
C	N	E	F	L	D	U	Z	Y	Y	W	G
H	T	R	H	M	G	F	I	E	L	D	R
C	A	S	T	L	E	H	C	O	A	S	T
O	I	J	S	T	A	T	I	O	N	C	R
D	N	Z	O	D	R	B	A	Y	S	L	K

sea – Meer, **harbour** – Hafen, **tower** – Turm,
square – Platz, **island** – Insel, **road** – Straße,
field – Feld/Sportplatz, **castle** – Schloss,
coast – Küste, **station** – Bahnhof, **bay** – Bucht,
hill – Hügel, **beach** – Strand, **mountain** – Berg,
lake – See, **canal** – Kanal

13 More about ... Orkney

1 islands 2 on, 3 biggest, 4 and, 5 but,
6 under, 7 another, 8 between, 9 takes,
10 for, 11 make, 12 history

14 The best word

1 exciting, 2 strange, 3 upset, 4 huge,
5 uncool, 6 realistic, 7 surprised

15 The fourth word

1 twice, *2* allowed to, *3* departure, *4* feeling,
5 stupid, *6* forgotten, *7* below, *8* translation

16 Vocabulary network

SCHOOL
do: a test, a project on Scotland, homework
work: alone, in a small group,
with a partner
listen to: the CD, an explanation, a recording
SPORTS
play: football, hockey, tennis
go: swimming, riding, surfing
do: judo, sport, yoga
HOBBIES AND FREE TIME
play: the drums, the piano, the trumpet
collect: model cars, postcards, stamps
visit: a friend, grandma, museums

Unit 3

1 What are the words?

1 information – is, *2* homework was,
3 is – hair, *4* transport – isn't,
5 wasn't – furniture, *6* is – news

2 The fourth word

1 once, *2* harbour, *3* beef, *4* vegetable,
5 in, *6* furniture, *7* blow, *8* instrument

3 Hidden words

1 nose, *2* singer, *3* east, *4* sea, *5* stone,
6 train, *7* star, *8* rain, *9* orange, *10* great,
11 art

4 Word families

a) *2* begin, *3* explain, *4* feel, *5* mean, *6* mix,
    7 move, *8* murder, *9* phone, *10* practise,
    11 bully, *12* invite, *13* teach, *14* translate
b) *1* meaning – explain, *2* invitation – invite,
    3 practise, *4* phone – arrive, *5* translation

5 Word friends

enter: a building, a room, a shop
score: again, three goals, a point
spot: a mistake, a fire, a hair in the soup
support: my school team, the players, the coach
train: at a sports club, hard, twice a week

6 Words in pictures

a) *1* face, *2* eye, *3* nose, *4* ear, *5* teeth,
    6 hair, *7* mouth, *8* finger, *9* hand
b) *1* pretty/round, *2* blue/bright,
    3 long/small, *4* my left/right,
    5 broken/white, *6* grey/tidy,
    7 a big/loud, *8* clean/strong

7 Definitions

1 washes – hair: **hairdresser**
2 looks – person: **clone**
3 team – matches: **supporter**
4 last – winner: **final**
5 sofas – sit: **furniture**
6 most – school: **head teacher**
7 country – pigs: **farmer**
8 unhappy – alone: **lonely**

8 Word ladder

need – **feed** – **feet** – **meet** – **meat** – **beat** – **boat** –
boot – **book** – **took** – **cook** – **look** – **lock** – luck

9 Last letter – first letter

1 stress, *2* support, *3* train, *4* news, *5* shirt,
6 travel, *7* leotard, *8* draw, *9* words,
10 salt, *11* tights, *12* stadium, *13* meaning,
14 goalkeeper, *15* realistic

10 Pronunciation

ə – colour, famous, harbour, nervous
aʊ – around, blouse, house, proud
uː – group, soup, through, you
ʌ – cousin, double, enough, touch
ɔː – bought, course, yours, thought

11 Crossword

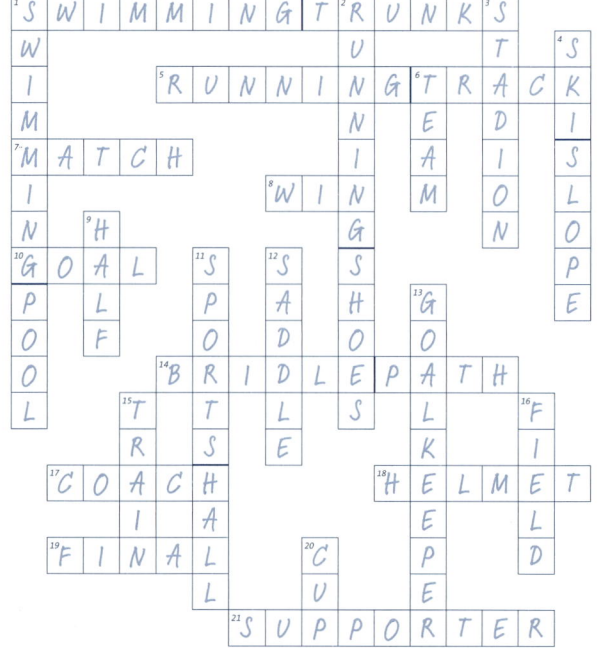

12 More about ... Manchester United

1 club, *2* times, *3* third, *4* over, *5* millions, *6* rich, *7* players, *8* huge, *9* match, *10* even, *11* than, *12* learn

13 Hour glasses

	1	S	P	Y		
2	S	P	O	O	N	
3	R	U	L	E	R	
4	S	H	I	R	T	
	5	I	C	E		
			E			
	6	T	W	O		
7	S	C	O	R	E	
8	R	O	M	A	N	
9	T	R	A	I	N	
	10	E	N	D		

	1	W	H	O		
2	C	O	A	C	H	
3	P	R	I	Z	E	
4	H	U	R	R	Y	
	5	A	D	D		
			R			
	6	P	E	N		
7	U	P	S	E	T	
8	E	S	S	A	Y	
9	S	T	E	E	L	
	10	A	R	T		

Das geheime Wort lautet:
Englisch – hairdresser, Deutsch – Friseur/in

14 Verb forms

1 do – did – done
2 grow up – grew up – grown up
3 take – took – taken
4 draw – drew – drawn
5 fight – fought – fought
6 beat – beat – beaten
7 choose – chose – chosen
8 begin – began – begun
9 blow – blew – blown
10 cut – cut – cut
11 forget – forgot – forgotten
12 let – let – let
13 upset – upset – upset
14 catch – caught – caught

15 Word search

```
G H D S A U S A G E L O C B K R H N
O A A P E V O L L E Y B A L L R E K
A M K A S C O U R T J S S O E X L N
L B S R A P L A N E F T T U S T I I
B U K A L S T A D I U M E S H R C U
O R I L A J W G S O C K W E E A O T
T G R Y D Z B L S G S K I S L M P I
R E T M U W Y B U S J A X F F Y T G
O R S P F U N D E R G R O U N D E H
U F O I T M C Z C S M S G R A U R T
S S U C T E M X H O W Q P N T W P S
E H P S A D S R I F K X C I H A G V
R O Q B D A H W P A F T H T L R Z F
S R X E J L O M S S G A A U E D T E
J T S D S X E M C H N B I R T R A R
Y S P A G H E T T I B L R E I O X R
Q P I Z Z A K U I P U E G O C B I Y
K C U R T A I N A N O R A K S E N E
```

room
bed, chair, curtain, furniture, shelf, sofa, table, wardrobe
clothes
anorak, blouse, shoe, shorts, skirt, sock, tights, trousers
transport
bus, ferry, helicopter, plane, ship, taxi, tram, underground
sport
athletics, court, goal, medal, Paralympics, skis, stadium, volleyball
food
chips, hamburger, pizza, salad, sausage, soup, spaghetti, stew

Unit 4

1 Lost words

1 at, *2* below, *3* on, *4* until, *5* above, *6* to, *7* about, *8* onto, *9* across, *10* about

2 School words

1 board, *2* choir, *3* class, *4* students, *5* history, *6* biology, *7* pencil, *8* teacher, *9* art, *10* essay
Das geheime Wort lautet:
Englisch – dictionary, Deutsch – Wörterbuch

3 Word pairs

build – stadium, **call** – ambulance,
climb – mountain, **cook** – stew,
correct – mistake, **grow** – lettuce,
listen to – live music, **read** – magazine,
score – goal, **turn on** – light,
wear – leotard, **win** – medal

4 One or two letters?

reggae, begin, language, biggest, fog, foggy
cellphone, adult, until, talent, model, pullover
community, swimmer, woman, grammar, moment, thermometer
population, shopping, pepper, supporter, represent, disappear
tomorrow, married, guitar, tired, hurry, directions
escape, essay, glasses, guess, husband, island
bottle, water, pretty, weather, spaghetti

5 Vocabulary network

TRAVEL
visit: a castle, an old church, a museum
pack: a suitcase, a bag, a rucksack
go: by train, on holiday, on a boat trip
SPORT AND FREE TIME
win: a cup, a medal, a prize
go: canoeing, fishing, snowshoeing
wear: running shoes, a helmet, pads
NOT WELL
feel: terrible, ill, weak
have: a sore throat, a cold, a temperature
phone: an ambulance, a doctor, the hospital

6 Spot the mistakes

1 childs: children, has: have
2 realy: really, off: of
3 allso: also, danger: dangerous
4 usualy: usually, errly: early
5 ran: run, swimers: swimmers
6 interresting: interesting, salmons: salmon
7 stand: stands, quitely: quietly
8 bare: bear, jump: jumps

7 Word search

```
R A B B I T H Y C H U I B G B
L N R O N P E W H O C C T I U
T W F G P N D H I R D R U R D
I U R S A M G A C S Y O R A G
G S W A R O E M K E X C K F I
E N F L R L H S E L P O E F E
R A R M O E O T N E I D Y E S
K K O O T P G E U P G I X F Q
Q E G N P C I R S H Q L C O U
R K A N G A R O O A I E O X I
H B W N Z F L I O N Q S W Y R
I E S W A L R U S T A H J U R
N A K W O O D P E C K E R S E
O R F S M O U S E R A E L U L
M O N K E Y G O W H I P P O W
```

8 Pronunciation

k: knee, knife
n: autumn, column
l: folk music, salmon
b: climb, lamb
w: answer, whole
c: scene, science

9 Words with different

1 **square** – Platz/Quadrat-,
2 **colour** – ausmalen/Farbe,
3 **train** – Zug/trainieren,
4 **date** – Datum/Verabredung,

5 **once** – einmal/einst,
6 **final** – Endspiel/letzte,
7 **argument** – Streit/Begründung

10 Odd word out

1 minute, 2 lyrics, 3 minus, 4 text message,
5 build, 6 sledges, 7 gig, 8 bottle

11 The fourth word

1 kilometre, 2 leader, 3 themselves,
4 number, 5 instrument, 6 year, 7 moon,
8 knives

12 More about ...traditional Inuit hunting

1 temperatures, 2 much, 3 fishing, 4 land,
5 just, 6 kind, 7 used, 8 could, 9 built,
10 plus

13 Number crossword

Provinz – **m** across, Hütte – **h** down,
Jagd – **o** across, Angriff – **j** across,
Erwachsene(r) – **p** across, schützen – **a** across,
streng – **e** down, Einwohnerzahl – **f** down

14 Word groups

jobs
actor, cleaner, farmer, painter, shop assistant,
waiter
music
choir, chorus, lyrics, instrument, concert,
song
station
suitcases, toilets, timetable, ticket machines,
railway, platforms, trains
weather
cloudy, fog, rain, snow, stormy, sunny,
tornado

15 Opposites

1 intolerant, *2* disagree, *3* modern, *4* up,
5 minus, *6* leave, *7* bottom, *8* remember,
9 departures, *10* wife, *11* boring, *12* cold,
13 dirty, *14* upstairs

Unit 5

1 Pronunciation

ʊ – bully, full, pull, put, push, sugar
juː – computer, community, excuse, huge,
    menu, tube
ʌ – fun, gun, publish, summer, tunnel,
    trumpet

2 Last letter – first letter

1 chorus, *2* success, *3* successful, *4* leader,
5 rapids, *6* spelling, *7* grandma, *8* announce,
9 editor, *10* revise, *11* electric, *12* crazy,
13 ja, *14* section

3 The fourth word

1 vegetable, *2* dish, *3* bird, *4* furniture,
5 instrument, *6* planet, *7* colour, *8* art

4 Making phrases

1 settle, *2* turn, *3* warn, *4* believe,
5 disagree, *6* grow, *7* look, *8* escape

5 Word building

1 bold print: Fettdruck
2 black bear: Schwarzbär
3 chat room: Chatroom
4 running shoes: Laufschuhe, Sportschuhe
5 text message: SMS
6 semi-final: Halbfinale
7 great-grandfather: Urgroßvater
8 classroom: Klassenzimmer, Klassenraum
9 snowshoes: Schneeschuhe
10 wheelchair: Rollstuhl

6 Word families

1 announce, *2* revise, *3* spell, *4* draw, *5* end,
6 live, *7* attack, *8* support, *9* hunt, *10* rap

7 Hour glasses

1	A	D	D
2	Q U E E N
3	U P S E T
4	F A C T S
5	T R Y
	I
6	S P Y
7	U N T I L
8	Q U I E T
9	P R O O F
10	E N D

1	A T E
2	D I R T Y
3	B E A C H
4	M E D A L
5	K I D
	T
6	B I N
7	C H O I R
8	F I N A L
9	S T A G E
10	I L L

Das geheime Wort lautet:
Englisch – traditional, Deutsch traditionell

8 Word ladder

size – **side** – **tide** – **hide** – **ride** – **rude** – **rule** –
role – **hole** – **mole** – **mile** – **mine** – **line** – **fine** –
file – film

9 Definitions

1 ears – radio: headphones
2 stop – more: strike
3 spend – home: sleepover
4 corrects – texts: editor
5 desks – work: office
6 picture – pen: drawing
7 goes – result: success
8 everybody – noise: silence

10 Words in pictures: fruit and vegetables

1 bright, red, tomatoes
2 delicious, forest, mushrooms
3 sweet, Spanish, oranges
4 hard, green, apples
5 big, garden, onions
6 delicious, German, strawberries
7 bright, orange, carrots
8 healthy, green, lettuce
9 delicious, new, potatoes
10 long, yellow, bananas

11 Opposites

1 worst, *2* bad, *3* top, *4* dark, *5* unhealthy,
6 old-fashioned, *7* late, *8* untidy, *9* behind,
10 answer, *11* below, *12* arrival, *13* right,
14 forget

12 The best word

1 final, *2* strict, *3* artificial, *4* silly, *5* relaxed,
6 useful

13 Hidden words

1 cinema, *2* listen, *3* tram, *4* castle *5* scan,
6 tunnel, *7* uncle, *8* mice, *9* sister,
10 summer/autumn, *11* clean

14 Word search – The media

S	N	E	W	S	P	A	P	E	R	C	I
T	H	R	H	O	L	G	D	H	M	K	T
A	Y	E	E	C	H	A	N	N	E	L	E
T	C	P	A	R	E	C	O	R	D	M	L
I	E	O	D	M	A	G	A	Z	I	N	E
O	L	R	P	E	D	I	T	O	R	M	V
N	L	T	H	C	G	S	Q	G	U	E	I
N	P	R	O	G	R	A	M	M	E	H	S
B	H	N	N	A	R	T	I	C	L	E	I
C	O	X	E	L	B	N	E	W	S	O	O
M	N	G	S	P	U	B	L	I	S	H	N
E	E	X	Q	G	M	O	N	I	T	O	R

newspaper – Zeitung
channel – Kanal/Sender
record – aufnehmen/Schallplatte
magazine – Zeitschrift
editor – Redakteur
programme – Programm
article – Artikel
news – Nachrichten
publish – veröffentlichen
monitor – Bildschirm/Monitor
station – Sender
cellphone – Handy/Mobiltelefon
report – Bericht
headphones – Kopfhörer
television – Fernsehen

15 Word friends

1 revise, *2* produce, *3* make, *4* record, *5* play,
6 go, *7* be, *8* have, *9* laugh, *10* skim

16 Scrambled words: American and British English

1 mom, mum, *2* cellphone, mobile,
3 elevator, lift *4* subway, underground
5 vacation, holidays

17 Crossword